378

W9-CHB-142

Poems of Robert Burns

THE CROWELL POETS
Under the editorship of Lillian Morrison

POEMS OF WILLIAM BLAKE
Selected by Amelia H. Munson

POEMS OF ROBERT BROWNING
Selected by Rosemary Sprague

POEMS OF ROBERT BURNS
Selected by Lloyd Frankenberg

POEMS OF LORD BYRON
Selected by Horace Gregory

POEMS OF SAMUEL TAYLOR COLERIDGE
Selected by Babette Deutsch

POEMS OF STEPHEN CRANE
Selected by Gerald D. McDonald

POEMS OF EMILY DICKINSON
Selected by Helen Plotz

POEMS OF RALPH WALDO EMERSON
Selected by J. Donald Adams

POEMS OF W. S. GILBERT
Selected by William Cole

POEMS OF ROBERT HERRICK
Selected by Winfield Townley Scott

POEMS OF JOHN KEATS
Selected by Stanley Kunitz

POEMS OF HENRY WADSWORTH LONGFELLOW
Selected by Edmund Fuller

POEMS OF EDGAR ALLAN POE
Selected by Dwight Macdonald

POEMS OF WILLIAM SHAKESPEARE
Selected by Lloyd Frankenberg

POEMS OF PERCY BYSSHE SHELLEY
Selected by Leo Gurko

POEMS OF ALFRED, LORD TENNYSON
Selected by Ruth Greiner Rausen

POEMS OF WALT WHITMAN
Selected by Lawrence Clark Powell

POEMS OF WILLIAM WORDSWORTH
Selected by Elinor Parker

POEMS OF
ROBERT BURNS

SELECTED BY LLOYD FRANKENBERG

Drawings by Joseph Low

Thomas Y. Crowell Company · New York

Table of Contents

———

SCOTCH, SCOTTISH, AND SCOTS

An Introduction to Robert Burns

Robert Burns was a Scotch poet who was not only a Scottish poet, but a true Scots poet. At the risk of infuriating a native of Scotland, this has for outlanders three degrees of meaning, more emotional than literal. Burns was a poet of Scotland who was not only native to Scotland, but imbued with pride in Scotland.

He is descended—if poetry may be thought of genealogically—from poets like William Dunbar, Allan Ramsay, and Robert Fergusson, who are Scottish, sometimes Scots, but never Scotch. Any interest there may be in their poetry is largely confined to Scotland itself and has seldom spread to those outlying regions of the English-speaking world for whom everything Scottish is imprecisely thought of as Scotch.

Why is Burns the culmination and exception? Despite the difficulties of penetrating his "Scotch dialect," he has been read more widely than any other Scottish writer except perhaps Sir Walter Scott and James M. Barrie. And they wrote, for the most part, in "English" English.

Perhaps one reason is his motive for writing. He gives it in the rhymed letter to his friend James Smith of Mauchline.

Some rhyme, he says, to get even for a grudge—"a neibor's name to lash." Others rhyme to make money—"(vain thought!)"—or to gain notoriety, "to court the countra clash, / And raise a din." As for himself, he has none of these aims in mind. "I rhyme for fun."

"Fun" may seem a slighting word to describe Burns's best poems. They are full of exuberance, a delight in everything that comes their way. They celebrate the everyday, disregarded occurrences of country life: a mouse's nest turned up while ploughing, the drinking of ale, the kissing of a girl in a rye field, the ascent of a lowly insect to the crown of a lofty bonnet.

All these celebrations are in the words that come most naturally to the poet, in his native dialect. When he strays from Scots, he is apt to become tiresomely "serious," to base his writings on inferior models, to express sentiments that are not truly his own.

"O heart-felt raptures! bliss beyond compare!" he exclaims in that tedious "classic," "The Cotter's Saturday Night." The rapture is spoken, but not present.

To appreciate his real flavor, it is worth the effort of "translating," for example, "Wee, sleekit, cowrin, tim'rous beastie" or "Dear Smith, the slee'st pawkie thief."

Significantly enough, in that poem to sly Smith, "fun" makes a half rhyme with "din." Long before Wilfred Owen, who deliberately experimented in this vein, and W. H. Auden, who raised the experiment to a degree of technical perfection, Burns's use seems impromptu, a result of impatience. He wants to get on with the poem and not stick over trifles. This gives his poems an air of improvisation, as if they were being composed as you read them.

So, in the same poem, "nature" will rhyme with "stature" and "feature," "lot" with "coat," "betters" with "tatters," and "heed" with "thread." And in another ("Ay, Waukin, O") he will go so far as to put "lover" to "colour" and "greetin" to "sleepin." All this with the inevitability of folk song, or such a nursery rhyme as "Jack and Jill went up the hill / To fetch a pail of water. / Jack fell down and broke his crown / And Jill came tumbling after." (Children are apt to be purists, and I can remember being greatly disturbed by the "bad rhyming" of "water" and "after.")

Especially in the various epistles to his friends, and indeed throughout his vernacular poems, Burns is the easy master of a colloquial, conversational, intensely personal style. When he addresses the devil, it is from no superior height. When he tries to console a mouse for having disrupted her nest, it is on terms of equality. True, he knows exactly where they differ. The mouse, lucky creature, has no anticipation; therefore, no fear of the future. But Burns explains all this, so simply and so without condescension, that by the end of the poem you feel sure the mouse must understand.

Even the louse, a personage perhaps the least endearing of Burns's creature friends, is not deprived of personality. "Ha! Whaur ye gaun?" demands Burns, not without a trace of admiration. One is reminded of Don Marquis' affection for his typewriter friend. "I see things from the underside," says archy the cockroach; and indeed he has a very special slant on life, if he never quite scales the heights of Burns's louse, climbing the giddy pinnacle of "Miss's fine Lunardi." (See the Glossary for a fuller appreciation of this particular eminence.)

It is humor, an ever-present sense of proportion, that forms the base from which Burns's poems take off. They do "take off"; they are never grounded to the matter-of-fact, sensible world. On the contrary, they turn the tables on it.

If his great fantasy, "Tam o' Shanter," begins prosaically enough with Tam having a wee bit too much to drink ("O'er a' the ills o' life victorious"), it proceeds to a very graphic, realistic description of a devil's dance. We may think this dance merely the product of Tam's overheated condition. But not so. Suffering the nearest of narrow

3

escapes, Tam arrives home to find that his mare Meg—who has taken never a drop the whole night—has only a stump for a tail. So the shreds of reality confirm the truth of imagination.

One is reminded of the speed with which satyrs and centaurs leap through the poems of a later master of gaiety, the Irish James Stephens. Sudden disappearance is the convincing proof of their existence.

The world of poetry abounds in paradox. Burns's life begins and ends on a note of tragedy. A week after his birth, January 25, 1759, at Alloway, Scotland, a storm blew down the clay house his father had built. And Burns's early death, July 21, 1796, was hastened by his falling asleep in a snowbank the preceding winter.

Robert Burns was the eldest of the seven children of William and Agnes (Broun or Brown) Burnes—as his father spelled it; for a time Robert signed himself Burness. William was a gardener and tenant-farmer, continually in difficulties with his proprietors. Lawsuits and long hours taxed his never very rugged strength, and did little to improve the rather frail health of his son. But Robert did receive the best education his father's limited means could provide.

One would scarcely recognize the later celebrator of carefree love from the way he addresses one of his early sweethearts, Ellison Begbie: "I verily believe, my dear E., that the pure genuine feelings of love are as rare in the world as the pure genuine principles of virtue and piety." And he goes on, in a tone almost as sanctimonious as what he later came to satirize in "The Holy Fair" and "Address to the Unco Guid."

Her rejection of his suit brought him to one of the lowest ebbs of his life. "I am quite transported," he wrote his father when he was twenty-two, "at the thought that ere long, perhaps very soon, I shall bid an eternal adieu to all the pains, and uneasinesses, and disquietudes of this weary life."

He had left home to learn the craft of flax-weaving, an apprenticeship that ended when the shop in which he was working burned down after a New Year's Eve celebration. As to his love affairs, they suddenly became too numerous to keep track of. Because of them, he was continually in hot water with the church, even the liberal wing with which his family was associated. Eventually he married the mother of four of his children, Jean Armour, and seems to have been happy with her despite any number of extra-marital involvements.

Around the year 1785 he began pouring forth what he calls "aye rowth o' rhymes." In two or three years he produced an impressive array of his best verse. At the same time, his affairs were in such desperate straits that he was about to emigrate to Jamaica, in 1786, when the publication of his poems in Edinburgh suddenly made him famous. He was feted all over Scotland. From this time dates the rather garish "legend" of Robert Burns, almost as lurid for its time as that of the Welsh poet Dylan Thomas in recent years.

The drinking prowess and amatory adventures have no doubt been exaggerated; yet there is too much basis in fact to justify the opposite extremes of opinion. The truth is apt to lie nearer to the remark of a friend and early commentator on Burns, Robert Heron: "He suffered himself to be surrounded by a race of miserable beings who were proud to tell that they had been in company with Burns, and had seen Burns as loose and foolish as themselves."

Burns had, almost to the point of affliction, the power to charm all that met him. Sir Walter Scott, who as a boy saw

Burns in Edinburgh, wrote later that he had never seen such an eye as Burns's "in a human head, though I have seen the most distinguished men of my time." Burns was, when he had it, prodigal of money, and his tours of Scotland exhausted most of the funds he made on his books. Because of this he was grateful, later, to receive employment as an exciseman, which entailed journeying up to two hundred miles a week in a rather hateful occupation. Among other things, Burns was expected to report anyone who made or sold illicit whiskey. His own scorn of this calling is reflected in the song, "The Deil's Awa wi' th' Exciseman." Other songs of the period were so outspokenly, if vaguely, "anti-government" that he was frequently in trouble with his superiors.

Burns's lifework divides itself, almost neatly, into two phases: first, the original poems, satires, epistles, epitaphs, epigrams that he wrote on his own account; second, the songs he later collected, as a labor of love, for James Johnson's *Scots Musical Museum* and George Thomson's *Select Collection of Original Scottish Airs*. Most of these consisted of traditional tunes that Burns remembered from his childhood, or picked up here and there, plus lyrics that he supplied himself or adapted from versions already existing in the rough.

Some of these songs are among the most beautiful in the language. From a suggestion ("O, wat, wat, / O, wat and weary, / Sleep I can get nane / For thinking o' my dearie.") comes the full-fledged inspiration of

> *Ay waukin, O,*
> *Waukin still and weary !*
> *Sleep I can get nane*
> *For thinking on my dearie.*

Similar subtle changes converted "Auld Lang Syne" and other tentative beginnings by earlier, sometimes anonymous poets into the classics we know today.

In the seventeenth century George Herbert set his own hymns to the lute—unfortunately the music is lost—but it is rare for a poet to set words to already-existing tunes and shows an exceptionally well-developed musical ear, as well as an ear for the music of words. This, Burns had to an extraordinary degree.

It was not, however, by any means infallible. Just as his heart is perennially on his sleeve, so his tongue is constantly framing "sentiments" that, by repetition, grow cloying. If it is difficult to submit to

> *An' O my Eppie,*
> *My jewel, my Eppie !*
> *Wha wadna be happy*
> *Wi' Eppie Adair ?*

what is one to say, a few pages on, to "O, saw ye my dearie, my Eppie Macnab?"

Even more incongruous are some of his excursions into "genteel manners." One of his presumably platonic affairs in Edinburgh was with Mrs. Agnes Maclehose, whom he addressed as "Clarinda," signing his verses to her, "Sylvander." To be just, they are among the posthumous poems and don't represent his own choice as to what should be included in a book.

Compare with them his "Holy Willie's Prayer," "The Holy Fair," and dozens of other poems in his own vein, and he is seen to be the most gifted poet produced by the Scots. He owed much, as he acknowledged, to the earlier attempts by poets like Fergusson, but he gave to the world much more than he took from them.

Considering Burns's "place" in poetry—an always

7

hazardous speculation—I am inclined to put him high among the writers of light verse. The word "light" may seem disparaging, implying an absence of weight or substance. But I am thinking of merriment and high spirits, no trivial accomplishments. In this sense Robert Herrick and Andrew Marvell are light. The Shakespeare of the songs and poems is light. In our own day Wallace Stevens, despite the complexity of his style and the urbanity of his manner, is witty and light.

Robert Burns sometimes takes himself—half-seriously—too seriously, as when he refers to "his bardship." But he never loses sight of the true source of his genius. When he is on the road toward "The Holy Fair," he meets "three hizzies." Greeting the liveliest of the three (the other two are "Superstition" and "Hypocrisy"), he is told:

My name is Fun—your cronie dear,
The nearest friend ye hae.

LLOYD FRANKENBERG

Aye Rowth o' Rhymes

———

TO A MOUSE

On Turning Her up in Her Nest with the Plough,
November 1785

W<small>EE</small>, sleekit, cowrin, tim'rous beastie,
O, what a panic's in thy breastie!
Thou need na start awa sae hasty,
     Wi' bickering brattle!
I wad be laith to rin an' chase thee,
     Wi' murd'ring pattle!

I'm truly sorry man's dominion,
Has broken nature's social union,
An' justifies that ill opinion,
     Which makes thee startle
At me, thy poor, earth-born companion,
     An' fellow-mortal!

I doubt na, whyles, but thou may thieve;
What then? poor beastie, thou maun live!
A daimen icker in a thrave
     'S a sma' request;
I'll get a blessin wi' the lave,
     An' never miss't!

Thy wee bit housie, too, in ruin!
It's silly wa's the win's are strewin!
An' naething, now, to big a new ane,
     O' foggage green!
An' bleak December's winds ensuin,
     Baith snell an' keen!

Thou saw the fields laid bare an' waste,
An' weary winter comin fast,
An' cozie here, beneath the blast,
      Thou thought to dwell—
Till crash! The cruel coulter past
      Out thro' thy cell.

That wee bit heap o' leaves an' stibble,
Has cost thee mony a weary nibble!
Now thou's turn'd out, for a' thy trouble,
      But house or hald,
To thole the winter's sleety dribble,
      An' cranreuch cauld!

But Mousie, thou art no thy lane,
In proving foresight may be vain;
The best-laid schemes o' mice an' men
      Gang aft agley,
An' lea'e us nought but grief an' pain,
      For promis'd joy!

Still thou art blest, compar'd wi' me!
The present only toucheth thee:
But och! I backward cast my e'e,
      On prospects drear!
An' forward, tho' I canna see,
      I guess an' fear!

TO A LOUSE

On Seeing One on a Lady's Bonnet at Church

Ha! whaur ye gaun, ye crowlin ferlie?
Your impudence protects you sairly;
I canna say but ye strunt rarely,
        Owre gauze and lace;
Tho', faith! I fear ye dine but sparely
        On sic a place.

Ye ugly, creepin, blastit wonner,
Detested, shunn'd by saunt an' sinner,
How daur ye set your fit upon her—
        Sae fine a lady?
Gae somewhere else and seek your dinner
        On some poor body.

Swith! in some beggar's haffet squattle;
There ye may creep, and sprawl, and sprattle,
Wi' ither kindred, jumping cattle,
        In shoals and nations;
Whaur horn nor bane ne'er daur unsettle
        Your thick plantations.

Now haud you there, ye're out o' sight,
Below the fatt'rels, snug and tight;
Na, faith ye yet! ye'll no be right,
        Till ye've got on it—
The verra tapmost, tow'rin height
        O' Miss's bonnet.

My sooth! right bauld ye set your nose out,
As plump an' grey as ony groset:
O for some rank, mercurial rozet,
              Or fell, red smeddum,
I'd gie you sic a hearty dose o't,
              Wad dress your droddum.

I wad na been surpris'd to spy
You on an auld wife's flainen toy;
Or aiblins some bit duddie boy,
              On's wyliecoat;
But Miss's fine Lunardi! fye!
              How daur ye do't?

O Jeany, dinna toss your head,
An' set your beauties a' abread!
Ye little ken what cursèd speed
              The blastie's makin:
Thae winks an' finger-ends, I dread,
              Are notice takin.

O wad some Power the giftie gie us
To see oursels as ithers see us!
It wad frae mony a blunder free us,
              An' foolish notion:
What airs in dress an' gait wad lea'e us,
              An' ev'n devotion!

THE TOAD-EATER

WHAT of earls with whom you have supped,
　　And of dukes that you dined with yestreen?
Lord! a louse, sir, is still but a louse,
　　Though it crawl on the curls of a queen.

TO A MOUNTAIN DAISY

On Turning One down with the Plough, in April 1786

WEE, modest, crimson-tippèd flow'r,
Thou's met me in an evil hour;
For I maun crush amang the stour
　　　　Thy slender stem;
To spare thee now is past my pow'r,
　　　　Thou bonie gem.

Alas! it's no thy neibor sweet,
The bonie lark, companion meet,
Bending thee 'mang the dewy weet,
　　　　Wi' spreckl'd breast!
When upward-springing, blythe, to greet
　　　　The purpling east.

Cauld blew the bitter-biting north
Upon thy early, humble birth;
Yet cheerfully thou glinted forth
            Amid the storm,
Scarce rear'd above the parent-earth
            Thy tender form.

The flaunting flow'rs our gardens yield,
High shelt'ring woods and wa's maun shield;
But thou, beneath the random bield
            O' clod or stane,
Adorns the histie stibble field,
            Unseen, alane.

There, in thy scanty mantle clad,
Thy snawie bosom sun-ward spread,
Thou lifts thy unassuming head
            In humble guise;
But now the share uptears thy bed,
            And low thou lies!

Such is the fate of artless maid,
Sweet flow'ret of the rural shade!
By love's simplicity betray'd,
            And guileless trust;
Till she, like thee, all soil'd, is laid
            Low i' the dust.

Such is the fate of simple bard,
On life's rough ocean luckless starr'd!
Unskilful he to note the card
            Of prudent lore,
Till billows rage, and gales blow hard,
            And whelm him o'er!

Such fate to suffering worth is giv'n,
Who long with wants and woes has striv'n,
By human pride or cunning driv'n
                    To mis'ry's brink;
Till wrench'd of ev'ry stay but Heav'n,
                    He, ruin'd, sink!

Ev'n thou who mourn'st the Daisy's fate,
That fate is thine—no distant date;
Stern Ruin's plough-share drives elate,
                    Full on thy bloom,
Till crush'd beneath the furrow's weight,
                    Shall be thy doom!

THE DEATH AND DYING WORDS
OF POOR MAILIE

The Author's Only Pet Yowe | An Unco Mournfu' Tale

———

As Mailie, an' her lambs thegither,
Was ae day nibbling on the tether,
Upon her cloot she coost a hitch,
An' owre she warsl'd in the ditch:
There, groaning, dying, she did lie,
When Hughoc he cam doytin by.

　　Wi' glowrin een, and lifted han's
Poor Hughoc like a statue stan's;
He saw her days were near-hand ended,
But wae's my heart! he could na mend it!
He gapèd wide, but naething spak,
At length poor Mailie silence brak.

　　"O thou, whase lamentable face
Appears to mourn my woefu' case!
My dying words attentive hear,
An' bear them to my Master dear.

　　"Tell him, if e'er again he keep
As muckle gear as buy a sheep—
O, bid him never tie them mair,
Wi' wicked strings o' hemp or hair!
But ca' them out to park or hill,
An' let them wander at their will:
So may his flock increase, an' grow
To scores o' lambs, an' packs o' woo'!

"Tell him, he was a Master kin',
An' aye was guid to me an' mine;
An' now my dying charge I gie him,
My helpless lambs, I trust them wi' him.

"O, bid him save their harmless lives,
Frae dogs, an' tods, an' butchers' knives!
But gie them guid cow-milk their fill,
Till they be fit to fend themsel';
An' tent them duly, e'en an' morn,
Wi' taets o' hay an' ripps o' corn.

"An' may they never learn the gates
Of ither vile, wanrestfu' pets—
To slink thro' slaps, an' reave an' steal
At stacks o' pease, or stocks o' kail!

So may they, like their great forbears,
For mony a year come thro' the shears:
So wives will gie them bits o' bread,
An' bairns greet for them when they're dead.

   "My poor toop-lamb, my son an' heir,
O, bid him breed him up wi' care!
An' if he live to be a beast,
To pit some havins in his breast!
An' warn him—what I winna name—
To stay content wi' yowes at hame;
An' no to rin an' wear his cloots,
Like ither menseless, graceless brutes.

   "An' neist, my yowie, silly thing,
Gude keep thee frae a tether string!
O, may thou ne'er forgather up,
Wi' ony blastit, moorland toop;
But aye keep mind to moop an' mell,
Wi' sheep o' credit like thysel'!

   "And now, my bairns, wi' my last breath,
I lea'e my blessin wi' you baith:
An' when you think upo' your mither,
Mind to be kind to ane anither.

   "Now, honest Hughoc, dinna fail,
To tell my master a' my tale;
An' bid him burn this cursed tether,
An' for thy pains thou'se get my blather."

   This said, poor Mailie turn'd her head,
An' closed her een amang the dead!

POOR MAILIE'S ELEGY

Lament in rhyme, lament in prose,
Wi' saut tears trickling down your nose;
Our bardie's fate is at a close,
                    Past a' remead!
The last, sad cape-stane o' his woes;
                    Poor Mailie's dead!

It's no the loss o' warl's gear,
That could sae bitter draw the tear,
Or mak our bardie, dowie, wear
                    The mourning weed:
He's lost a friend an' neebor dear
                    In Mailie dead.

Thro' a' the town she trotted by him;
A lang half-mile she could descry him;
Wi' kindly bleat, when she did spy him,
                    She ran wi' speed:
A friend mair faithfu' ne'er cam nigh him,
                    Than Mailie dead.

I wat she was a sheep o' sense,
An' could behave hersel' wi' mense:
I'll say't, she never brak a fence,
                    Thro' thievish greed.
Our bardie, lanely, keeps the spence
                    Sin' Mailie's dead.

Or, if he wanders up the howe,
Her livin image in her yowe

Comes bleating till him, owre the knowe,
        For bits o' bread;
An' down the briny pearls rowe
        For Mailie dead.

She was nae get o' moorland tips,
Wi' tauted ket, an' hairy hips;
For her forbears were brought in ships,
        Frae 'yont the Tweed.
A bonier fleesh ne'er cross'd the clips
        Than Mailie's dead.

Wae worth the man wha first did shape
That vile, wanchancie thing—a raip!
It maks guid fellows girn an' gape,
        Wi' chokin dread;
An' Robin's bonnet wave wi' crape
        For Mailie dead.

O a' ye bards on bonie Doon!
An' wha on Ayr your chanters tune!
Come, join the melancholious croon
        O' Robin's reed!
His heart will never get aboon—
        His Mailie's dead!

ADDRESS TO A HAGGIS

Fair fa' your honest, sonsie face,
Great chieftain o' the pudding-race!
Aboon them a' ye take your place,
                    Painch, tripe, or thairm:
Weel are ye wordy o' a grace
                    As lang's my arm.

The groaning trencher there ye fill,
Your hurdies like a distant hill,
Your pin wad help to mend a mill
                    In time o' need,
While thro' your pores the dews distil
                    Like amber bead.

His knife see rustic Labour dight,
An' cut you up wi' ready sleight,
Trenching your gushing entrails bright,
                    Like ony ditch;
And then, O what a glorious sight,
                    Warm-reekin, rich!

Then, horn for horn, they stretch an' strive:
Deil tak the hindmost! on they drive,
Till a' their weel-swall'd kytes belyve,
                    Are bent lyke drums;
Then auld Guidman, maist like to rive,
                    'Bethankit!' hums.

Is there that owre his French *ragout*
Or *olio* that wad staw a sow,

Or *fricassee* wad mak her spew
                    Wi' perfect sconner,
Looks down wi' sneering, scornfu' view
                    On sic a dinner?

Poor devil! see him owre his trash,
As feckless as a wither'd rash,
His spindle shank, a guid whip-lash,
                    His nieve a nit;
Thro' bloody flood or field to dash,
                    O how unfit!

But mark the Rustic, haggis-fed,
The trembling earth resounds his tread.
Clap in his walie nieve a blade,
                    He'll mak it whissle;
An' legs an' arms, an' heads will sned,
                    Like taps o' thrissle.

Ye Pow'rs wha mak mankind your care,
And dish them out their bill o' fare,
Auld Scotland wants nae skinking ware
                    That jaups in luggies;
But, if ye wish her gratefu' prayer,
                    Gie her a haggis!

EPITAPH ON JOHN DOVE, INNKEEPER

HERE lies Johnie Pigeon;
What was his religion
   Whae'er desires to ken,
To some other warl'
Maun follow the carl,
   For here Johnie Pigeon had nane.

Strong ale was ablution,
Small beer persecution,
   A dram was *memento mori;*
But a full-flowing bowl
Was the saving his soul,
   And port was celestial glory.

JOHN BARLEYCORN: A BALLAD

THERE was three kings into the east,
   Three kings both great and high,
And they hae sworn a solemn oath
   John Barleycorn should die.

They took a plough and plough'd him down,
   Put clods upon his head,
And they hae sworn a solemn oath
   John Barleycorn was dead.

But the cheerful Spring came kindly on,
　　And show'rs began to fall,
John Barleycorn got up again,
　　And sore surpris'd them all.

The sultry suns of Summer came,
　　And he grew thick and strong;
His head weel arm'd wi' pointed spears,
　　That no one should him wrong.

The sober Autumn enter'd mild,
　　When he grew wan and pale;
His bending joints and drooping head
　　Show'd he began to fail.

His colour sicken'd more and more,
　　He faded into age;
And then his enemies began
　　To show their deadly rage.

They've taen a weapon, long and sharp,
　　And cut him by the knee;
Then tied him fast upon a cart,
　　Like a rogue for forgerie.

They laid him down upon his back,
　　And cudgell'd him full sore;
They hung him up before the storm,
　　And turn'd him o'er and o'er.

They fillèd up a darksome pit
　　With water to the brim;
They heavèd in John Barleycorn,
　　There let him sink or swim.

They laid him out upon the floor,
   To work him further woe;
And still, as signs of life appear'd,
   They toss'd him to and fro.

They wasted, o'er a scorching flame,
   The marrow of his bones;
But a miller us'd him worst of all,
   For he crush'd him between two stones.

And they hae taen his very heart's blood,
   And drank it round and round;
And still the more and more they drank,
   Their joy did more abound.

John Barleycorn was a hero bold,
   Of noble enterprise;
For if you do but taste his blood,
   'Twill make your courage rise.

'Twill make a man forget his woe;
   'Twill heighten all his joy;
'Twill make the widow's heart to sing,
   Tho' the tear were in her eye.

Then let us toast John Barleycorn,
   Each man a glass in hand;
And may his great posterity
   Ne'er fail in old Scotland!

EPISTLE TO JAMES SMITH

Friendship, mysterious cement of the soul!
Sweet'ner of Life, and solder of Society!
I owe thee much——

— BLAIR

DEAR SMITH, the slee'st, pawkie thief,
That e'er attempted stealth or rief!
Ye surely hae some warlock-brief
        Owre human hearts;
For ne'er a bosom yet was prief
        Against your arts.

For me, I swear by sun an' moon,
An' ev'ry star that blinks aboon,
Ye've cost me twenty pair o' shoon,
        Just gaun to see you;
An' ev'ry ither pair that's done,
        Mair taen I'm wi' you.

That auld, capricious carlin, Nature,
To mak amends for scrimpit stature,
She's turn'd you off, a human creature
        On her first plan,
And in her freaks, on ev'ry feature
        She's wrote the Man.

Just now I've taen the fit o' rhyme,
My barmie noddle's working prime,
My fancy yerkit up sublime,
        Wi' hasty summon;
Hae ye a leisure-moment's time
        To hear what's comin?

Some rhyme a neibor's name to lash;
Some rhyme (vain thought!) for needfu' cash;
Some rhyme to court the countra clash,
                    An' raise a din;
For me, an aim I never fash;
                    I rhyme for fun.

The star that rules my luckless lot,
Has fated me the russet coat,
An' damn'd my fortune to the groat;
                    But, in requit,
Has blest me with a random-shot
                    O' countra wit.

This while my notion's taen a sklent,
To try my fate in guid, black prent;
But still the mair I'm that way bent,
                    Something cries "Hoolie!
I red you, honest man, tak tent!
                    Ye'll shaw your folly;

There's ither poets, much your betters,
Far seen in Greek, deep men o' letters,
Hae thought they had ensur'd their debtors,
                    A' future ages;
Now moths deform, in shapeless tatters,
                    Their unknown pages."

Then farewell hopes of laurel-boughs,
To garland my poetic brows!
Henceforth I'll rove where busy ploughs
                    Are whistlin thrang,
An' teach the lanely heights an' howes
                    My rustic sang.

I'll wander on, wi' tentless heed
How never-halting moments speed,
Till fate shall snap the brittle thread;
            Then, all unknown,
I'll lay me with th' inglorious dead,
            Forgot and gone!

But why o' death begin a tale?
Just now we're living sound and hale;
Then top and maintop crowd the sail,
            Heave Care o'er-side!
And large, before Enjoyment's gale,
            Let's tak the tide.

This life, sae far's I understand,
Is a' enchanted fairy-land,
Where Pleasure is the magic-wand,
            That, wielded right,
Maks hours like minutes, hand in hand,
            Dance by fu' light.

The magic-wand then let us wield;
For ance that five-an'-forty's speel'd,
See, crazy, weary, joyless eild,
            Wi' wrinkl'd face,
Comes hostin, hirplin owre the field,
            Wi' creepin pace.

When ance life's day draws nears the gloamin,
Then fareweel vacant, careless roamin;
An' fareweel cheerfu' tankards foamin,
            An' social noise:
An' fareweel dear, deluding woman,
            The joy of joys!

O Life! how pleasant, in thy morning,
Young Fancy's rays the hills adorning!
Cold-pausing Caution's lesson scorning,
          We frisk away,
Like school-boys, at th' expected warning,
          To joy an' play.

We wander there, we wander here,
We eye the rose upon the brier,
Unmindful that the thorn is near,
          Among the leaves;
And tho' the puny wound appear,
          Short while it grieves.

Some, lucky, find a flow'ry spot,
For which they never toil'd nor swat;
They drink the sweet and eat the fat,
          But care or pain;
And haply eye the barren hut
          With high disdain.

With steady aim, some fortune chase;
Keen hope does ev'ry sinew brace;
Thro' fair, thro' foul, they urge the race,
          An' seize the prey:
Then cannie, in some cozie place,
          They close the day.

And others, like your humble servan',
Poor wights! nae rules nor roads observin,
To right or left eternal swervin,
          They zig-zag on;
Till, curst with age, obscure an' starvin,
          They aften groan.

Alas! what bitter toil an' straining—
But truce with peevish, poor complaining!
Is fortune's fickle *Luna* waning?
   E'en let her gang!
Beneath what light she has remaining,
   Let's sing our sang.

My pen I here fling to the door,
And kneel, ye Pow'rs! and warm implore,
"Tho' I should wander *Terra* o'er,
   In all her climes,
Grant me but this, I ask no more,
   Aye rowth o' rhymes.

"Gie dreepin roasts to countra lairds,
Till icicles hing frae their beards;
Gie fine braw claes to fine life-guards,
   And maids of honour;
An' yill an' whisky gie to cairds,
   Until they sconner.

"A title, Dempster merits it;
A garter gie to Willie Pitt;
Gie wealth to some be-ledger'd cit,
   In cent. per cent.;
But give me real, sterling wit,
   And I'm content.

"While ye are pleas'd to keep me hale,
I'll sit down o'er my scanty meal,
Be't water-brose or muslin-kail,
   Wi' cheerfu' face,
As lang's the Muses dinna fail
   To say the grace."

An anxious e'e I never throws
Behint my lug, or by my nose;
I jouk beneath Misfortune's blows
                    As weel's I may;
Sworn foe to sorrow, care and prose,
                    I rhyme away.

O ye douce folk that live by rule,
Grave, tideless-blooded, calm an' cool,
Compar'd wi' you—O fool! fool! fool!
                    How much unlike!
Your hearts are just a standing pool,
                    Your lives, a dyke!

Nae hair-brained, sentimental traces
In your unletter'd, nameless faces!
In *arioso* trills and graces
                    Ye never stray;
But *gravissimo*, solemn basses
                    Ye hum away.

Ye are sae grave, nae doubt ye're wise;
Nae ferly tho' ye do despise
The hairum-scairum, ram-stam boys,
                    The rattling squad:
I see ye upward cast your eyes—
                    Ye ken the road!

Whilst I—but I shall haud me there,
Wi' you I'll scarce gang ony where—
Then, Jamie, I shall say nae mair,
                    But quat my sang,
Content wi' you to mak a pair
                    Whare'er I gang.

ON THE DUCHESS OF GORDON'S
REEL DANCING

She kiltit up her kirtle weel
  To show her bonie cutes sae sma',
And wallopèd about the reel,
  The lightest louper o' them a'!

While some, like slav'ring, doited stots
  Stoit'ring out thro' the midden dub,
Fankit their heels amang their coats
  And gart the floor their backsides rub,

Gordon, the great, the gay, the gallant,
  Skip't like a maukin owre a dyke:
Deil tak me, since I was a callant,
  Gif e'er my een beheld the like!

ADDRESS TO THE TOOTHACHE

My curse upon your venom'd stang,
That shoots my tortur'd gooms alang,
An' thro' my lug gies monie a twang,
          Wi' gnawing vengeance,
Tearing my nerves wi' bitter pang,
          Like racking engines!

A' down my beard the slavers trickle,
I throw the wee stools o'er the mickle,
While round the fire the giglets keckle,
        To see me loup,
An', raving mad, I wish a heckle
        Were i' their doup!

When fevers burn, or ague freezes,
Rheumatics gnaw, or colic squeezes,
Our neibor's sympathy may ease us,
        Wi' pitying moan;
But thee!—thou hell o' a' diseases—
        They mock our groan.

Of a' the numerous human dools,
Ill hairsts, daft bargains, cutty-stools,
Or worthy frien's rak'd i' the mools—
        Sad sight to see!
The tricks o' knaves, or fash o' fools,
        Thou bear'st the gree!

Whare'er that place be priests ca' hell,
Whare a' the tones o' misery yell,
An' rankèd plagues their numbers tell,
        In dreadfu' raw,
Thou, Toothache, surely bear'st the bell,
        Amang them a'!

O thou grim, mischief-making chiel,
That gars the notes o' discord squeel,
Till daft mankind aft dance a reel
        In gore, a shoe-thick,
Gie a' the faes o' Scotland's weal
        A towmond's toothache!

HOLY WILLIE'S PRAYER

And send the godly in a pet to pray. —POPE

———————

O THOU, that in the heavens does dwell,
Wha, as it pleases best Thysel',
Sends ane to heaven an' ten to hell,
      A' for thy glory,
And no for onie guid or ill
      They've done afore Thee!

I bless and praise Thy matchless might,
When thousands Thou hast left in night,
That I am here afore Thy sight,
      For gifts an' grace
A burning and a shining light
      To a' this place.

What was I, or my generation,
That I should get sic exaltation,
I wha deserv'd most just damnation
      For broken laws,
Sax thousand years ere my creation,
      Thro' Adam's cause.

When from my mither's womb I fell,
Thou might hae plung'd me deep in hell,
To gnash my gooms, and weep and wail,
      In burnin lakes,
Where damnèd devils roar and yell,
      Chain'd to their stakes.

Yet I am here a chosen sample,
To show thy grace is great and ample;
I'm here a pillar o' Thy temple,
      Strong as a rock,
A guide, a buckler, and example,
      To a' Thy flock.

O Lord, Thou kens what zeal I bear,
When drinkers drink, an' swearers swear,
An' singing here, an' dancin' there,
      Wi' great and sma';
For I am keepit by Thy fear
      Free frae them a'.

But yet, O Lord! confess I must,
At times I'm fash'd wi' fleshly lust:
An' sometimes, too, in warldly trust,
      Vile self gets in;
But Thou remembers we are dust,
      Defil'd wi' sin.

O Lord! yestreen, Thou kens, wi' Meg—
Thy pardon I sincerely beg;
O! may't ne'er be a livin plague
      To my dishonour,
An' I'll ne'er lift a lawless leg
      Again upon her.

Besides, I farther maun allow,
Wi' Leezie's lass, three times I trow—
But Lord, that Friday I was fou,
      When I cam near her;
Or else, Thou kens, Thy servant true
      Wad never steer her.

Maybe Thou lets this fleshly thorn
Buffet Thy servant e'en and morn,
Lest he owre proud and high shou'd turn,
   That he's sae gifted:
If sae, Thy han' maun e'en be borne,
   Until Thou lift it.

Lord, bless Thy chosen in this place,
For here Thou has a chosen race:
But God confound their stubborn face,
   An' blast their name,
Wha bring Thy elders to disgrace
   An' public shame.

Lord, mind Gaw'n Hamilton's deserts;
He drinks, an' swears, an' plays at cartes,
Yet has sae mony takin arts,
   Wi' great and sma',
Frae God's ain priest the people's hearts
   He steals awa.

An' when we chasten'd him therefor,
Thou kens how he bred sic a splore,
An' set the warld in a roar
   O' laughing at us;—
Curse Thou his basket and his store,
   Kail an' potatoes.

Lord, hear my earnest cry and pray'r,
Against that Presbyt'ry o' Ayr;
Thy strong right hand, Lord, make it bare
   Upo' their heads;
Lord, visit them, an' dinna spare,
   For their misdeeds.

O Lord, my God! that glib-tongu'd Aiken,
My vera heart and flesh are quakin,
To think how we stood sweatin, shakin,
          An' pish'd wi' dread,
While he, wi' hingin lip an' snakin,
          Held up his head.

Lord, in Thy day o' vengeance try him,
Lord, visit them wha did employ him,
And pass not in Thy mercy by them,
          Nor hear their pray'r,
But for thy people's sake destroy them,
          An' dinna spare.

But, Lord, remember me an' mine
Wi' mercies temporal and divine,
That I for grace an' gear may shine,
          Excell'd by nane,
And a' the glory shall be thine,
          Amen, Amen!

EPITAPH ON HOLY WILLIE

Here Holy Willie's sair worn clay
    Taks up its last abode;
His saul has ta'en some other way,
    I fear, the left-hand road.

Stop! there he is, as sure's a gun,
    Poor, silly body, see him;
Nae wonder he's as black's the grun,
    Observe wha's standing wi' him.

Your brunstane devilship, I see,
    Has got him there before ye;
But haud your nine-tail cat a wee,
    Till ance you've heard my story.

Your pity I will not implore,
    For pity ye have nane;
Justice, alas! has gi'en him o'er,
    And mercy's day is gane.

But hear me, Sir, deil as ye are,
    Look something to your credit;
A coof like him wad stain your name,
    If it were kent ye did it.

ELEGY ON WILLIE NICOL'S MARE

PEG NICHOLSON was a good bay mare,
  As ever trod on airn;
But now she's floating down the Nith,
  And past the mouth o' Cairn.

Peg Nicholson was a good bay mare,
  An' rode thro' thick an' thin;
But now she's floating down the Nith,
  And wanting even the skin.

Peg Nicholson was a good bay mare,
  And ance she bore a priest!
But now she's floating down the Nith,
  For Solway fish a feast.

Peg Nicholson was a good bay mare,
  An' the priest he rode her sair;
And much oppress'd, and bruis'd she was,
  As priest-rid cattle are.

ON DR. BABINGTON'S LOOKS

THAT there is falsehood in his looks,
  I must and will deny:
They say their Master is a knave,
  And sure they do not lie.

THE HOLY FAIR

A robe of seeming truth and trust
    Hid crafty observation;
And secret hung, with poison'd crust,
    The dirk of defamation:
A mask that like the gorget show'd,
    Dye-varying on the pigeon;
And for a mantle large and broad,
    He wrapt him in *Religion*.
                    —HYPOCRISY A-LA-MODE

Upon a simmer Sunday morn,
    When Nature's face is fair,
I walkèd forth to view the corn,
    An' snuff the caller air.
The rising sun owre Galston muirs
    Wi' glorious light was glinting;
The hares were hirplin down the furrs,
    The lav'rocks they were chantin
                    Fu' sweet that day.

As lightsomely I glowr'd abroad,
    To see a scene sae gay,
Three hizzies, early at the road,
    Cam skelpin up the way.
Twa had manteeles o' dolefu' black,
    But ane wi' lyart lining;
The third, that gaed a wee a-back,
    Was in the fashion shining
                    Fu' gay that day.

The twa appear'd like sisters twin,
    In feature, form, an' claes;
Their visage wither'd, lang an' thin,
    An' sour as ony slaes:

The third cam up, hap-stap-an'-lowp,
   As light as ony lambie,
An' wi' a curchie low did stoop,
   As soon as e'er she saw me,
         Fu' kind that day.

Wi' bonnet aff, quoth I, "Sweet lass,
   I think ye seem to ken me;
I'm sure I've seen that bonie face,
   But yet I canna name ye."
Quo' she, an' laughin as she spak,
   An' taks me by the han's,
"Ye, for my sake, hae gien the feck
   Of a' the ten comman's
         A screed some day.

"My name is Fun—your cronie dear,
   The nearest friend ye hae;
An' this is Superstition here,
   An' that's Hypocrisy.
I'm gaun to Mauchline 'holy fair,'
   To spend an hour in daffin:
Gin ye'll go there, yon runkl'd pair,
   We will get famous laughin
         At them this day."

Quoth I, "Wi' a' my heart, I'll do't;
   I'll get my Sunday's sark on,
An' meet you on the holy spot;
   Faith, we'se hae fine remarkin!"
Then I gaed hame at crowdie-time,
   An' soon I made me ready;
For roads were clad, frae side to side,
   Wi' mony a weary body
         In droves that day.

Here farmers gash, in ridin graith,
   Gaed hoddin by their cotters;
There swankies young, in braw braid-claith,
   Are springing owre the gutters.
The lasses, skelpin barefit, thrang,
   In silks an' scarlets glitter;
Wi' sweet-milk cheese, in mony a whang,
   An' farls, bak'd wi' butter,
                    Fu' crump that day.

When by the plate we set our nose,
   Weel heapèd up wi' ha'pence,
A greedy glow'r black-bonnet throws,
   An' we maun draw our tippence.
Then in we go to see the show:
   On ev'ry side they're gath'rin;
Some carrying dails, some chairs an' stools,
   An' some are busy bleth'rin
                    Right loud that day.

Here stands a shed to fend the show'rs,
   An' screen our countra gentry;
There "Racer Jess," an' twa-three whores,
   Are blinking at the entry.
Here sits a raw o' tittlin jads,
   Wi' heaving breast an' bare neck;
An' there a batch o' wabster lads,
   Blackguarding frae Kilmarnock,
                    For fun this day.

Here some are thinkin on their sins,
   An' some upo' their claes;
Ane curses feet that fyl'd his shins,
   Anither sighs an' prays:
On this hand sits a chosen swatch,

Wi' screw'd-up, grace-proud faces;
On that a set o' chaps, at watch,
 Thrang winkin on the lasses
   To chairs that day.

O happy is that man, an' blest!
 Nae wonder that it pride him?
Whase ain dear lass, that he likes best,
 Comes clinkin down beside him!
Wi' arm repos'd on the chair back,
 He sweetly does compose him;
Which, by degrees, slips round her neck,
 An's loof upon her bosom,
   Unkend that day.

Now a' the congregation o'er
 Is silent expectation;
For Moodie speels the holy door,
 Wi' tidings o' damnation:
Should *Hornie*, as in ancient days,
 'Mang sons o' God present him,
The vera sight o' Moodie's face,
 To 's ain het hame had sent him
   Wi' fright that day.

Hear how he clears the points o' Faith
 Wi' rattlin and wi' thumpin!
Now meekly calm, now wild in wrath,
 He's stampin, an' he's jumpin!
His lengthen'd chin, his turned-up snout,
 His eldritch squeel an' gestures,
O how they fire the heart devout,
 Like cantharidian plaisters
   On sic a day!

But hark! the tent has chang'd its voice
    There's peace an' rest nae langer;
For a' the real judges rise,
    They canna sit for anger;
Smith opens out his cauld harangues,
    On practice and on morals;
An' aff the godly pour in thrangs,
    To gie the jars an' barrels
            A lift that day.

What signifies his barren shine,
    Of moral powers an' reason?
His English style, an' gesture fine,
    Are a' clean out o' season.
Like Socrates or Antonine,
    Or some auld pagan heathen,
The *moral man* he does define,
    But ne'er a word o' *faith* in
            That's right that day.

In guid time comes an antidote
    Against sic poison'd nostrum;
For Peebles, frae the water-fit,
    Ascends the holy rostrum:
See, up he's got the word o' God,
    An' meek an' mim has view'd it,
While Common-sense has taen the road,
    An' aff, an' up the Cowgate
            Fast, fast that day.

Wee Miller neist the guard relieves,
    An' Orthodoxy raibles,
Tho' in his heart he weel believes
    An' thinks it auld wives' fables:
But faith! the birkie wants a manse,

So, cannilie he hums them;
Altho' his carnal wit an' sense
    Like hafflins-wise o'ercomes him
        At times that day.

Now butt an' ben the change-house fills,
    Wi' yill-caup commentators;
Here's crying out for bakes and gills,
    An' there the pint-stowp clatters;
While thick an' thrang, an' loud an' lang,
    Wi' logic and wi' scripture,
They raise a din, that in the end
    Is like to breed a rupture
        O' wrath that day.

Leeze me on drink! it gies us mair
    Than either school or college;
It kindles wit, it waukens lear,
    It pangs us fou o' knowledge:
Be't whisky-gill or penny wheep,
    Or ony stronger potion,
It never fails, on drinkin deep,
    To kittle up our notion,
        By night or day.

The lads and lassies, blythely bent
    To mind baith saul an' body,
Sit round the table, weel content,
    An' steer about the toddy:
On this ane's dress, an' that ane's leuk,
    They're makin observations;
While some are cozy i' the neuk,
    An' forming assignations
        To meet some day.

But now the Lord's ain trumpet touts,
    Till a' the hills are rairin,
And echoes back return the shouts;
    Black Russell is na sparin:
His piercin words, like Highlan' swords,
    Divide the joints an' marrow:
His talk o' Hell, where devils dwell,
    Our vera "sauls does harrow"
                Wi' fright that day!

A vast, unbottom'd, boundless pit,
    Fill'd fou o' lowin brunstane,
Whase raging flame, an' scorching heat,
    Wad melt the hardest whun-stane!
The half-asleep start up wi' fear,
    An' think they hear it roarin;
When presently it does appear,
    'Twas but some neibor snorin
                Asleep that day.

'Twad be owre lang a tale to tell,
    How monie stories past;
An' how they crouded to the yill,
    When they were a' dismist;
How drink gaed round, in cogs and caups,
    Amang the furms and benches;
An' cheese an' bread, frae women's laps,
    Was dealt about in lunches
                An' dawds that day.

In comes a gawsie, gash guidwife,
    An' sits down by the fire,
Syne draws her kebbuck an' her knife;
    The lasses they are shyer:
The auld guidmen, about the grace,

Frae side to side they bother;
Till some ane by his bonnet lays,
An' gies them't, like a tether,
Fu' lang that day.

Waesucks! for him that gets nae lass,
Or lasses that hae naething!
Sma' need has he to say a grace,
Or melvie his braw claithing!
O wives, be mindfu' ance yoursel'
How bonie lads ye wanted;
An' dinna for a kebbuck-heel
Let lasses be affronted
On sic a day!

Now Clinkumbell, wi' rattlin tow,
Begins to jow an' croon;
Some swagger hame the best they dow,
Some wait the afternoon.
At slaps the billies halt a blink,
Till lasses strip their shoon:
Wi' faith an' hope, an' love an' drink,
They're a' in famous tune
For crack that day.

How mony hearts this day converts
O' sinners and o' lasses!
Their hearts o' stane, gin night, are gane
As saft as ony flesh is:
There's some are fou o' love divine;
There's some are fou o' brandy;
An' mony jobs that day begin,
May end in houghmagandie
Some ither day.

ADDRESS TO THE UNCO GUID

or the Rigidly Righteous

My Son, these maxims make a rule,
    An' lump them aye thegither;
The *Rigid Righteous* is a fool,
    The *Rigid Wise* anither:
The cleanest corn that ere was dight
    May hae some pyles o' caff in;
So ne'er a fellow creature slight
    For random fits o' daffin.
              SOLOMON—Eccles. 7:16

———————

O YE wha are sae guid yoursel',
    Sae pious and sae holy,
Ye've nought to do but mark and tell
    Your neibours' fauts and folly!
Whase life is like a weel-gaun mill,
    Supplied wi' store o' water;
The heapèd happer's ebbing still,
    An' still the clap plays clatter.

Hear me, ye venerable core,
    As counsel for poor mortals
That frequent pass douce Wisdom's door
    For glaikit Folly's portals:
I, for their thoughtless, careless sakes,
    Would here propone defences—
Their donsie tricks, their black mistakes,
    Their failings and mischances.

Ye see your state wi' theirs compared,
    And shudder at the niffer;
But cast a moment's fair regard,
    What maks the mighty differ?

Discount what scant occasion gave,
    That purity ye pride in;
And (what's aft mair than a' the lave)
    Your better art o' hidin.

Think, when your castigated pulse
    Gies now and then a wallop,
What ragings must his veins convulse,
    That still eternal gallop!
Wi' wind and tide fair i' your tail,
    Right on ye scud your sea-way;
But in the teeth o' baith to sail,
    It maks an unco lee-way.

See Social Life and Glee sit down,
    All joyous and unthinking,
Till, quite transmugrified, they're grown
    Debauchery and Drinking:
O would they stay to calculate
    Th' eternal consequences;
Or your more dreaded hell to state,
    Damnation of expenses!

Ye high, exalted, virtuous dames,
    Tied up in godly laces,
Before ye gie poor Frailty names,
    Suppose a change o' cases;
A dear-lov'd lad, convenience snug,
    A treach'rous inclination—
But let me whisper i' your lug,
    Ye're aiblins nae temptation.

Then gently scan your brother man,
    Still gentler sister woman;

Tho' they may gang a kennin wrang,
  To step aside is human;
One point must still be greatly dark,—
  The moving *Why* they do it;
And just as lamely can ye mark,
  How far perhaps they rue it.

Who made the heart, 'tis He alone
  Decidedly can try us;
He knows each chord, its various tone,
  Each spring, its various bias;
Then at the balance let's be mute,
  We never can adjust it;
What's done we partly may compute,
  But know not what's resisted.

ADDRESS TO THE DEIL

O Prince! O chief of many thronèd pow'rs
That led th' embattl'd seraphim to war—
—MILTON

O Thou! whatever title suit thee—
Auld Hornie, Satan, Nick, or Clootie,
Wha in yon cavern grim an' sootie,
        Clos'd under hatches,
Spairges about the brunstane cootie,
        To scaud poor wretches!

Hear me, auld Hangie, for a wee,
An' let poor damnèd bodies be;
I'm sure sma' pleasure it can gie,
        Ev'n to a deil,
To skelp an' scaud poor dogs like me,
        An' hear us squeel!

Great is thy pow'r an' great thy fame;
Far ken'd an' noted is thy name;
An' tho' yon lowin' heugh's thy hame,
        Thou travels far;
An' faith! thou's neither lag nor lame,
        Nor blate, nor scaur.

Whyles, ranging like a roarin lion,
For prey, a' holes and corners tryin;
Whyles, on the strong-wing'd tempest flyin,
        Tirlin the kirks;
Whyles, in the human bosom pryin,
        Unseen thou lurks.

53

I've heard my rev'rend graunie say,
In lanely glens ye like to stray;
Or where auld ruin'd castles grey
                    Nod to the moon,
Ye fright the nightly wand'rer's way,
                    Wi' eldritch croon.

When twilight did my graunie summon,
To say her pray'rs, douse, honest woman!
Aft 'yont the dyke she's heard you bummin,
                    Wi' eerie drone;
Or, rustlin, thro' the boortrees comin,
                    Wi' heavy groan.

Ae dreary, windy, winter night,
The stars shot down wi' sklentin light,
Wi' you mysel' I gat a fright,
                    Ayont the lough;
Ye, like a rash-buss, stood in sight,
                    Wi' wavin sough.

The cudgel in my nieve did shake,
Each bristl'd hair stood like a stake,
When wi' an eldritch, stoor "quaick, quaick,"
                    Amang the springs,
Awa ye squatter'd like a drake,
                    On whistling wings.

Let warlocks grim, an' wither'd hags,
Tell how wi' you, on ragweed nags,
They skim the muirs an' dizzy crags,
                    Wi' wicked speed;
And in kirk-yards renew their leagues,
                    Owre howkit dead.

Thence countra wives, wi' toil and pain,
May plunge an' plunge the kirn in vain;
For oh! the yellow treasure's ta'en
         By witchin skill;
An' dawtit, twal-pint hawkie's gane
         As yell's the bill.

Thence mystic knots mak great abuse
On young guidmen, fond, keen an' crouse
When the best wark-lume i' the house,
         By cantrip wit,
Is instant made no worth a louse,
         Just at the bit.

When thowes dissolve the snawy hoord,
An' float the jinglin icy boord,
Then water-kelpies haunt the foord,
        By your direction,
And 'nighted trav'lers are allur'd
           To their destruction.

And aft your moss-traversin Spunkies
Decoy the wight that late an' drunk is:
The bleezin, curst, mischievous monkies
        Delude his eyes,
Till in some miry slough he sunk is,
          Ne'er mair to rise.

When masons' mystic word an' grip
In storms an' tempest raise you up,
Some cock or cat your rage maun stop,
        Or, strange to tell!
The youngest brither ye wad whip
         Aff straught to hell.

Lang syne in Eden's bonie yard,
When youthfu' lovers first were pair'd,
An' all the soul of love they shar'd,
        The raptur'd hour,
Sweet on the fragrant flow'ry swaird,
         In shady bower;

Then you, ye auld, snick-drawing dog!
Ye cam to Paradise incog,
An' play'd on man a cursèd brogue,
        (Black be your fa'!)
An' gied the infant warld a shog,
        'Maist ruin'd a'.

D'ye mind that day when in a bizz
Wi' reekit duds, an' reestit gizz,
Ye did present your smoutie phiz
         'Mang better folk
An' sklented on the man of Uzz
           Your spitefu' joke?

An' how ye gat him i' your thrall,
An' brak him out o' house an hal',
While scabs and botches did him gall,
           Wi' bitter claw;
An' lows'd his ill-tongu'd wicked scaul',
           Was warst ava?

But a' your doings to rehearse,
Your wily snares an' fechtin fierce,
Sin' that day Michael did you pierce,
           Down to this time,
Wad ding a Lallan tongue, or Erse,
           In prose or rhyme.

An' now auld Cloots, I ken ye're thinkin,
A certain bardie's rantin, drinkin,
Some luckless hour will send him linkin
           To your black pit;
But faith! he'll turn a corner jinkin,
           An' cheat you yet.

But fare-you-weel, auld Nickie-ben!
O wad ye tak a thought an' men'!
Ye aiblins might—I dinna ken—
           Still hae a stake:
I'm wae to think upo' yon den,
           Ev'n for your sake!

Tam o' Shanter

TAM O' SHANTER

A Tale

Of Brownyis and of Bogillis full is this Buke.
—GAWIN DOUGLAS

———

WHEN chapman billies leave the street,
And drouthy neibors neibors meet;
As market days are wearing late,
And folk begin to tak the gate,
While we sit bousing at the nappy,
An' getting fou and unco happy,
We think na on the lang Scots miles,
The mosses, waters, slaps and stiles,
That lie between us and our hame,
Where sits our sulky, sullen dame,
Gathering her brows like gathering storm,
Nursing her wrath to keep it warm.

This truth fand honest TAM O' SHANTER,
As he frae Ayr ae night did canter:
(Auld Ayr, wham ne'er a town surpasses,
For honest men and bonie lasses).

O Tam! hadst thou but been sae wise,
As taen thy ain wife Kate's advice!
She tauld thee weel thou was a skellum,
A blethering, blustering, drunken blellum;
That frae November till October,
Ae market-day thou was na sober;
That ilka melder wi' the Miller,
Thou sat as lang as thou had siller;

61

That ev'ry naig was ca'd a shoe on
The Smith and thee gat roarin fou on;
That at the Lord's house, ev'n on Sunday,
Thou drank wi' Kirkton Jean till Monday;
She prophesied that late or soon,
Thou wad be found, deep down'd in Doon,
Or catch'd wi' warlocks in the mirk,
By Alloway's auld, haunted kirk.

Ah, gentle dames! it gars me greet,
To think how mony counsels sweet,
How mony lengthen'd, sage advices,
The husband frae the wife despises!

But to our tale:—Ae market night,
Tam had got planted unco right,
Fast by an ingle, bleezing finely,
Wi' reaming swats that drank divinely;
And at his elbow, Souter Johnie,
His ancient, trusty, drouthy crony:
Tam lo'ed him like a very brither;
They had been fou for weeks thegither.
The night drave on wi' sangs an' clatter;
And aye the ale was growing better:
The Landlady and Tam grew gracious,
Wi' favours secret, sweet and precious:
The Souter tauld his queerest stories;
The Landlord's laugh was ready chorus:
The storm without might rair and rustle,
Tam did na mind the storm a whistle.

Care, mad to see a man sae happy,
E'en drown'd himsel amang the nappy.
As bees flee hame wi' lades o' treasure,

The minutes wing'd their way wi' pleasure:
Kings may be blest, but Tam was glorious,
O'er a' the ills o' life victorious!

But pleasures are like poppies spread,
You seize the flow'r, its bloom is shed;
Or like the snow falls in the river,
A moment white—then melts for ever;
Or like the Borealis race,
That flit ere you can point their place;
Or like the Rainbow's lovely form
Evanishing amid the storm.—
Nae man can tether Time nor Tide,
The hour approaches Tam maun ride;
That hour, o' night's black arch the key-stane,
That dreary hour he mounts his beast in;
And sic a night he taks the road in,
As ne'er poor sinner was abroad in.

The wind blew as 'twad blawn its last;
The rattling showers rose on the blast;
The speedy gleams the darkness swallow'd;
Loud, deep, and lang the thunder bellow'd:
That night, a child might understand,
The deil had business on his hand.

Weel-mounted on his grey mare Meg,
A better never lifted leg,
Tam skelpit on thro' dub and mire,
Despising wind, and rain, and fire;
Whiles holding fast his gude blue bonnet,
Whiles crooning o'er some auld Scots sonnet,
Whiles glow'rin round wi' prudent cares,
Lest bogles catch him unawares;
Kirk-Alloway was drawing nigh,
Where ghaists and houlets nightly cry.

By this time he was cross the ford,
Where in the snaw the chapman smoor'd;
And past the birks and meikle stane,
Where drunken Charlie brak's neck-bane;
And thro' the whins, and by the cairn,
Where hunters fand the murder'd bairn;
And near the thorn, aboon the well,
Where Mungo's mither hang'd hersel'.
Before him Doon pours all his floods,
The doubling storm roars thro' the woods,
The lightnings flash from pole to pole,
Near and more near the thunders roll,
When, glimmering thro' the groaning trees,
Kirk-Alloway seem'd in a bleeze,
Thro' ilka bore the beams were glancing,
And loud resounded mirth and dancing.

Inspiring bold John Barleycorn!
What dangers thou canst make us scorn!
Wi' tippenny, we fear nae evil;
Wi' usquebae, we'll face the devil!
The swats sae ream'd in Tammie's noddle,
Fair play, he car'd na deils a boddle,
But Maggie stood, right sair astonish'd,
Till, by the heel and hand admonish'd,
She ventur'd forward on the light;
And, wow! Tam saw an unco sight!

Warlocks and witches in a dance:
Nae cotillon, brent-new frae France,
But hornpipes, jigs, strathspeys, and reels,
Put life and mettle in their heels.
A winnock-bunker in the east,
There sat auld Nick, in shape o' beast;
A tousie tyke, black, grim, and large,
To gie them music was his charge:
He screw'd the pipes and gart them skirl,
Till roof and rafters a' did dirl.—
Coffins stood round, like open presses,
That shaw'd the Dead in their last dresses;
And (by some devilish cantraip sleight)
Each in its cauld hand held a light.
By which heroic Tam was able
To note upon the haly table,
A murderer's banes, in gibbet-airns;
Two span-lang, wee, unchristened bairns;
A thief, new-cutted frae a rape,
Wi' his last gasp his gab did gape;
Five tomahawks, wi' blude red-rusted;
Five scimitars, wi' murder crusted;
A garter which a babe had strangled;

A knife, a father's throat had mangled,
Whom his ain son of life bereft,
The grey hairs yet stack to the heft;
Wi' mair of horrible and awfu',
Which even to name wad be unlawfu'.
Three Lawyers' tongues, turned inside out,
Wi' lies seamed like a beggar's clout;
Three Priests' hearts, rotten, black as muck,
Lay stinking, vile, in every neuk.

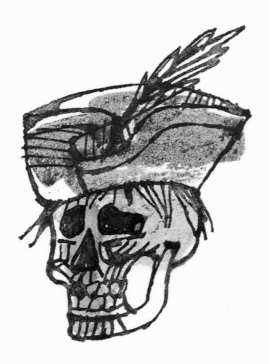

As Tammie glowr'd, amaz'd and curious,
The mirth and fun grew fast and furious;
The Piper loud and louder blew,
The dancers quick and quicker flew,
They reel'd, they set, they cross'd, they cleekit,
Till ilka carlin swat and reekit,
And coost her duddies to the wark,
And linkit at it in her sark!

Now Tam, O Tam! had they been queans,
A' plump and strapping in their teens!
Their sarks, instead o' creeshie flainen,
Been snaw-white seventeen-hunder linen!—
Thir breeks o' mine, my only pair,
That ance were plush, o' guid blue hair,
I wad hae gien them off my hurdies,
For ae blink o' the bonie burdies!
But wither'd beldams, auld and droll,
Rigwoodie hags wad spean a foal,
Louping an' flinging on a crummock,
I wonder did na turn thy stomach.

But Tam kent what was what fu' brawlie:
There was ae winsome wench and waulie
That night enlisted in the core,
Lang after ken'd on Carrick shore
(For mony a beast to dead she shot,
And perish'd mony a bonie boat,
And shook baith meikle corn and bear,
And kept the country-side in fear);
Her cutty sark, o' Paisley harn,
That while a lassie she had worn,
In longitude tho' sorely scanty,
It was her best, and she was vauntie.

Ah! little ken'd thy reverend grannie,
That sark she coft for her wee Nannie,
Wi' twa pund Scots ('twas a' her riches),
Wad ever grac'd a dance of witches!

But here my Muse her wing maun cour,
Sic flights are far beyond her power;
To sing how Nannie lap and flang
(A souple jade she was and strang),
And how Tam stood, like ane bewitch'd,
And thought his very een enrich'd:

Even Satan glowr'd, and fidg'd fu' fain,
And hotch'd and blew wi' might and main:
Till first ae caper, syne anither,
Tam tint his reason a' thegither,
And roars out, "Weel done, Cutty-sark!"
And in an instant all was dark:
And scarcely had he Maggie rallied,
When out the hellish legion sallied.

As bees bizz out wi' angry fyke,
When plundering herds assail their byke;
As open pussie's mortal foes,
When, pop! she starts before their nose;
As eager runs the market-crowd,
When "Catch the thief!" resounds aloud;
So Maggie runs, the witches follow,
Wi' mony an eldritch skreich and hollo.

Ah, Tam! Ah, Tam! thou'll get thy fairin!
In hell they'll roast thee like a herrin!
In vain thy Kate awaits thy comin!
Kate soon will be a woefu' woman!
Now, do thy speedy utmost, Meg,
And win the key-stane o' the brig;
There, at them thou thy tail may toss,
A running stream they dare na cross,
But ere the key-stane she could make,
The fient a tail she had to shake!
For Nannie, far before the rest,
Hard upon noble Maggie prest,
And flew at Tam wi' furious ettle;
But little wist she Maggie's mettle!
Ae spring brought off her master hale,
But left behind her ain grey tail:

The carlin claught her by the rump,
And left poor Maggie scarce a stump.

Now, wha this tale o' truth shall read,
Ilk man, and mother's son, take heed:
Whene'er to Drink you are inclin'd,
Or Cutty-sarks rin in your mind,
Think ye may buy the joys o'er dear;
Remember Tam o' Shanter's mare.

The Jolly Beggars

THE JOLLY BEGGARS

A Cantata

Recitativo

WHEN lyart leaves bestrow the yird,
Or wavering like the bauckie-bird,
  Bedim cauld Boreas' blast;
When hailstanes drive wi' bitter skyte,
And infant frosts begin to bite,
  In hoary cranreuch drest;
Ae night at e'en a merry core
  O' randie, gangrel bodies,
In Poosie-Nansie's held the splore,
  To drink their orra duddies;
    Wi' quaffing an' laughing,
      They ranted an' they sang,
    Wi' jumping an' thumping,
      The vera girdle rang.

First, neist the fire, in auld red rags,
Ane sat, weel brac'd wi' mealy bags,
  And knapsack a' in order;
His doxy lay within his arm;
Wi' usquebae an' blankets warm
  She blinkit on her sodger;
An' aye he gies the tozie drab
  The tither skelpin kiss,
While she held up her greedy gab,
  Just like an aumous dish;
    Ilk smack still did crack still,
      Just like a cadger's whip;
    Then staggering an' swaggering
      He roar'd this ditty up—

I am a son of Mars who have been in many wars,
    And show my cuts and scars wherever I come;
This here was for a wench, and that other in a trench,
    When welcoming the French at the sound of the drum.
        Lal de daudle, etc.

My prenticeship I past where my leader breath'd his last,
    When the bloody die was cast on the heights of Abram:
And I servèd out my trade when the gallant game was
    play'd,
    And the Moro low was laid at the sound of the drum.

I lastly was with Curtis among the floating batt'ries,
    And there I left for witness an arm and a limb;
Yet let my country need me, with Elliot to head me,
    I'd clatter on my stumps at the sound of a drum.

And now tho' I must beg, with a wooden arm and leg,
    And many a tatter'd rag hanging over my bum,
I'm as happy with my wallet, my bottle and my callet,
    As when I used in scarlet to follow a drum.

What tho', with hoary locks, I must stand the winter shocks,
    Beneath the woods and rocks oftentimes for a home,
When the tother bag I sell, and the tother bottle tell,
    I could meet a troop of hell, at the sound of a drum.

Recitativo
    He ended; and the kebars sheuk,
        Aboon the chorus roar;
    While frighted rattons backward leuk,
        An' seek the benmost bore:
    A fairy fiddler frae the neuk,

He skirl'd out, *Encore !*
But up arose the martial chuck,
   An' laid the loud uproar.

Song
I once was a maid, tho' I cannot tell when,
And still my delight is in proper young men:
Some one of a troop of dragoons was my daddie,
No wonder I'm fond of a sodger laddie.
   Sing, lal de lal, etc.

The first of my loves was a swaggering blade,
To rattle the thundering drum was his trade;
His leg was so tight, and his cheek was so ruddy,
Transported I was with my sodger laddie.

But the godly old chaplain left him in the lurch;
The sword I forsook for the sake of the church:
He ventur'd the soul, and I riskèd the body,
'Twas then I proved false to my sodger laddie.

Full soon I grew sick of my sanctified sot,
The regiment at large for a husband I got;
From the gilded spontoon to the fife I was ready,
I askèd no more but a sodger laddie.

But the peace it reduc'd me to beg in despair,
Till I met my old boy in a Cunningham fair;
His rags regimental, they flutter'd so gaudy,
My heart it rejoic'd at a sodger laddie.

And now I have liv'd—I know not how long,
And still I can join in a cup and a song;
But whilst with both hands I can hold the glass steady,
Here's to thee, my hero, my sodger laddie.

Recitativo

Poor Merry-Andrew, in the neuk,
　　Sat guzzling wi' a tinkler-hizzie;
They mind't na wha the chorus teuk,
　　Between themselves they were sae busy:
　　At length, wi' drink an' courting dizzy,
He stoiter'd up an' made a face;
　　Then turn'd an' laid a smack on Grizzie,
Syne tun'd his pipes wi' grave grimace.

Song
Sir Wisdom's a fool when he's fou;
   Sir Knave is a fool in a session;
He's there but a prentice I trow,
   But I am a fool by profession.

My grannie she bought me a beuk,
   An' I held awa to the school;
I fear I my talent misteuk,
   But what will ye hae of a fool?

77

For drink I would venture my neck;
 A hizzie's the half of my craft;
But what could ye other expect
 Of ane that's avowedly daft?

I ance was tied up like a stirk,
 For civilly swearing and quaffin;
I ance was abus'd i' the kirk,
 For towsing a lass i' my daffin.

Poor Andrew that tumbles for sport,
 Let naebody name wi' a jeer;
There's ev'n, I'm tauld, i' the Court
 A tumbler ca'd the Premier.

Observ'd ye yon reverend lad
 Mak faces to tickle the mob;
He rails at our mountebank squad,—
 It's rivalship just i' the job.

And now my conclusion I'll tell,
 For faith I'm confoundedly dry;
The chiel that's a fool for himsel',
 Guid Lord! he's far dafter than I.

Recitativo

Then niest out spak a raucle carlin,
Wha kent fu' weel to cleek the sterlin;
For monie a pursie she had hooked,
An' had in mony a well been douked:
Her love had been a Highland laddie,
But weary fa' the waeful woodie!
Wi' sighs and sobs she thus began
To wail her braw John Highlandman.

Song

A Highland lad my love was born,
The Lalland laws he held in scorn;
But he still was faithfu' to his clan,
My gallant, braw John Highlandman.

Chorus   Sing hey my braw John Highlandman!
Sing ho my braw John Highlandman!
There's not a lad in a' the lan'
Was match for my John Highlandman.

With his philibeg an' tartan plaid,
An' guid claymore down by his side,
The ladies' hearts he did trepan,
My gallant, braw John Highlandman,

We rangèd a' from Tweed to Spey,
An' liv'd like lords an' ladies gay;
For a Lalland face he fearèd none,—
My gallant, braw John Highlandman.

They banish'd him beyond the sea.
But ere the bud was on the tree,
Adown my cheeks the pearls ran,
Embracing my John Highlandman.

But, och! they catch'd him at the last,
And bound him in a dungeon fast:
My curse upon them every one,
They've hang'd my braw John Highlandman!

And now a widow, I must mourn
The pleasures that will ne'er return:

No comfort but a hearty can,
When I think on John Highlandman.

Recitativo
A pigmy scraper wi' his fiddle,
Wha us'd at trystes an' fairs to driddle,
Her strapping limb and gausy middle
      (He reach'd nae higher)
Had hol'd his heartie like a riddle,
      An' blawn't on fire.

Wi' hand on hainch, and upward e'e,
He croon'd his gamut, one, two, three,
Then in an *arioso* key,
      The wee Apollo
Set off wi' *allegretto* glee
      His *giga* solo.

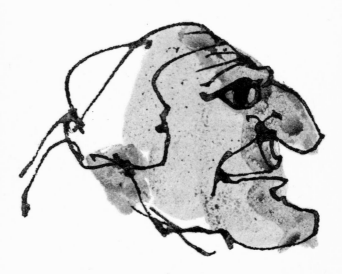

Song

Let me ryke up to dight that tear,
An' go wi' me an' be my dear;
An' then your every care an' fear
    May whistle owre the lave o't.

Chorus   I am a fiddler to my trade,
An' a' the tunes that e'er I played,
The sweetest still to wife or maid,
    Was whistle owre the lave o't.

At kirns an' weddins we'se be there,
An' O sae nicely's we will fare!
We'll bowse about till Daddie Care
    Sing whistle owre the lave o't.

Sae merrily's the banes we'll pyke,
An' sun oursel's about the dyke;
An' at our leisure, when ye like,
    We'll whistle owre the lave o't.

But bless me wi' your heav'n o' charms,
An' while I kittle hair on thairms,
Hunger, cauld, an' a' sic harms,
    May whistle owre the lave o't.

Recitativo

Her charms had struck a sturdy caird,
    As weel as poor gut-scraper;
He taks the fiddler by the beard,
    An' draws a roosty rapier—
He swoor by a' was swearing worth,
    To speet him like a pliver,

Unless he would from that time forth
  Relinquish her for ever.

Wi' ghastly e'e, poor tweedle-dee
  Upon his hunkers bended,
An' pray'd for grace wi' ruefu' face,
  An' so the quarrel ended.
But tho' his little heart did grieve,
  When round the tinkler prest her,
He feign'd to snirtle in his sleeve,
  When thus the caird address'd her:

Song

My bonie lass, I work in brass,
  A tinkler in my station:
I've travell'd round all Christian ground
  In this my occupation;
I've taen the gold, an' been enrolled
  In many a noble squadron;
But vain they search'd when off I march'd
  To go an' clout the cauldron.
                I've taen the gold, etc.

Despise that shrimp, that wither'd imp,
  With a' his noise an' cap'rin;
An' take a share with those that bear
  The budget and the apron!
And by that stowp! my faith an' houp,
  And by that dear Kilbaigie,
If e'er ye want, or meet wi' scant,
  May I ne'er weet my craigie.
                And by that stowp, etc.

Recitativo

The caird prevail'd—th' unblushing fair
   In his embraces sunk;
Partly wi' love o'ercome sae sair,
   An' partly she was drunk:
Sir Violino, with an air
   That show'd a man o' spunk,
Wish'd unison between the pair,
   An' made the bottle clunk
          To their health that night.

But hurchin Cupid shot a shaft,
    That play'd a dame a shavie—
The fiddler rak'd her, fore and aft,
    Behint the chicken cavie.
Her lord, a wight of Homer's craft,
    Tho' limpin wi' the spavie,
He hirpl'd up, an' lap like daft,
    An' shor'd them *Dainty Davie*
            O' boot that night.

He was a care-defying blade
    As ever Bacchus listed!
Tho' Fortune sair upon him laid,
    His heart, she ever miss'd it.
He had no wish but—to be glad,
    Nor want but—when he thirsted;
He hated nought but—to be sad,
    An' thus the muse suggested
            His sang that night.

Song
I am a Bard of no regard,
    Wi' gentle folks an' a' that;
But Homer-like, the glowrin byke,
    Frae town to town I draw that.

Chorus   For a' that, an' a' that,
        An' twice as muckle's a' that;
    I've lost but ane, I've twa behin',
        I've wife eneugh for a' that.

I never drank the Muses' stank,
    Castalia's burn, an' a' that;

But there it streams an' richly reams,
　　My Helicon I ca' that.

Great love I bear to a' the fair,
　　Their humble slave an' a' that;
But lordly will, I hold it still
　　A mortal sin to thraw that.

In raptures sweet, this hour we meet,
　　Wi' mutual love an' a' that;
But for how lang the flie may stang,
　　Let inclination law that.

Their tricks an' craft hae put me daft,
　　They've taen me in, an' a' that;
But clear your decks, and here's—"The Sex!"
　　I like the jads for a' that.

Chorus　　For a' that, an' a' that,
　　　　An' twice as muckle's a' that;
　　　　My dearest bluid, to do them guid,
　　　　They're welcome till't for a' that.

Recitativo

So sang the bard—and Nansie's wa's
Shook with a thunder of applause,
　　Re-echo'd from each mouth!
They toom'd their pocks, they pawn'd their duds,
They scarcely left to co'er their fuds,
　　To quench their lowin drouth:
Then owre again, the jovial thrang
　　The poet did request
To lowse his pack an' wale a sang,
　　A ballad o' the best;

He rising, rejoicing,
　　Between his twa Deborahs,
Looks round him, an' found them
　　Impatient for the chorus.

Song
See the smoking bowl before us,
　　Mark our jovial ragged ring!
Round and round take up the chorus,
　　And in raptures let us sing—

Chorus　　A fig for those by law protected!
　　　　　　Liberty's a glorious feast!
　　　　　Courts for cowards were erected,
　　　　　　Churches built to please the priest.

What is title, what is treasure,
　　What is reputation's care?
If we lead a life of pleasure,
　　'Tis no matter how or where!

With the ready trick and fable,
　　Round we wander all the day;
And at night in barn or stable,
　　Hug our doxies on the hay.

Does the train-attended carriage
　　Thro' the country lighter rove?
Does the sober bed of marriage
　　Witness brighter scenes of love?

Life is all a variorum,
　　We regard not how it goes;

Let them cant about decorum,
   Who have character to lose.

Here's to budgets, bags and wallets!
   Here's to all the wandering train.
Here's our ragged brats and callets,
   One and all cry out, Amen!

Chorus   A fig for those by law protected!
      Liberty's a glorious feast!
   Courts for cowards were erected,
      Churches built to please the priest.

"Gin a Body Kiss a Body"

A RED, RED ROSE

O MY luve's like a red, red rose,
   That's newly sprung in June:
O my luve's like the melodie,
   That's sweetly play'd in tune.

As fair art thou, my bonie lass,
   So deep in luve am I;
And I will luve thee still, my dear,
   Till a' the seas gang dry.

Till a' the seas gang dry, my dear,
   And the rocks melt wi' the sun;
And I will luve thee still, my dear,
   While the sands o' life shall run.

And fare-thee-weel, my only luve!
   And fare-thee-weel a while!
And I will come again, my luve,
   Tho' it were ten thousand mile.

MARY MORISON

O Mary, at thy window be,
  It is the wish'd, the trysted hour!
Those smiles and glances let me see,
  That make the miser's treasure poor:
How blythely wad I bide the stour,
  A weary slave frae sun to sun,
Could I the rich reward secure,
  The lovely Mary Morison.

Yestreen, when to the trembling string
  The dance gaed thro' the lighted ha',
To thee my fancy took its wing,
  I sat, but neither heard nor saw:
Tho' this was fair, and that was braw,
  And yon the toast of a' the town,
I sigh'd, and said amang them a',
  "Ye are na Mary Morison."

Oh, Mary, canst thou wreck his peace,
  Wha for thy sake wad gladly die?
Or canst thou break that heart of his,
  Whase only faut is loving thee?
If love for love thou wilt na gie,
  At least be pity to me shown;
A thought ungentle canna be
  The thought o' Mary Morison.

SWEET AFTON

FLOW gently, sweet Afton! among thy green braes,
Flow gently, I'll sing thee a song in thy praise;
My Mary's asleep by thy murmuring stream,
Flow gently, sweet Afton, disturb not her dream.

Thou stock dove whose echo resounds thro' the glen,
Ye wild whistling blackbirds in yon thorny den,
Thou green crested lapwing, thy screaming forbear,
I charge you, disturb not my slumbering Fair.

How lofty, sweet Afton, thy neighbouring hills,
Far mark'd with the courses of clear, winding rills;
There daily I wander as noon rises high,
My flocks and my Mary's sweet cot in my eye.

How pleasant thy banks and green valleys below,
Where, wild in the woodlands, the primroses blow;
There oft, as mild Ev'ning weeps over the lea,
The sweet-scented birk shades my Mary and me.

Thy crystal stream, Afton, how lovely it glides,
And winds by the cot where my Mary resides;
How wanton thy waters her snowy feet lave,
As, gathering sweet flowerets, she stems thy clear wave.

Flow gently, sweet Afton, among thy green braes,
Flow gently, sweet river, the theme of my lays;
My Mary's asleep by thy murmuring stream,
Flow gently, sweet Afton, disturb not her dream.

HIGHLAND MARY

Y E banks and braes and streams around
   The castle o' Montgomery!
Green be your woods, and fair your flowers,
   Your waters never drumlie:
There Simmer first unfald her robes,
   And there the langest tarry;
For there I took the last fareweel
   O' my sweet Highland Mary.

How sweetly bloom'd the gay, green birk,
   How rich the hawthorn's blossom,
As underneath their fragrant shade,
   I clasp'd her to my bosom!
The golden Hours on angel wings,
   Flew o'er me and my dearie;
For dear to me, as light and life,
   Was my sweet Highland Mary.

Wi' mony a vow, and lock'd embrace,
   Our parting was fu' tender;
And, pledging aft to meet again,
   We tore oursels asunder;
But O, fell Death's untimely frost,
   That nipt my flower sae early!
Now green's the sod, and cauld's the clay
   That wraps my Highland Mary!

O pale, pale now, those rosy lips,
   I aft hae kiss'd sae fondly!
And clos'd for aye, the sparkling glance

That dwalt on me sae kindly!
And mouldering now in silent dust,
That heart that lo'ed me dearly!
But still within my bosom's core
Shall live my Highland Mary.

MY HEART'S IN THE HIGHLANDS

———

Farewell to the Highlands, farewell to the North,
The birth-place of Valour, the country of Worth;
Wherever I wander, wherever I rove,
The hills of the Highlands for ever I love.

Chorus   My heart's in the Highlands, my heart is not here,
My heart's in the Highlands, a-chasing the deer;
A-chasing the wild-deer, and following the roe,
My heart's in the Highlands wherever I go.

Farewell to the mountains, high-cover'd with snow,
Farewell to the straths and green valleys below;
Farewell to the forests and wild-hanging woods,
Farewell to the torrents and loud-pouring floods.

THE BANKS O' DOON

Ye flowery banks o' bonie Doon,
   How can ye blume sae fair?
How can ye chant, ye little birds,
   And I sae fu' o' care!

Thou'll break my heart, thou bonie bird,
   That sings upon the bough!
Thou minds me o' the happy days
   When my fause luve was true.

Thou'll break my heart, thou bonie bird,
   That sings beside thy mate;
For sae I sat, and sae I sang,
   And wist na o' my fate.

Aft hae I rov'd by bonie Doon,
   To see the woodbine twine;
And ilka bird sang o' its luve,
   And sae did I o' mine.

Wi' lightsome heart I pu'd a rose,
   Upon its thorny tree;
But my fause luver staw my rose,
   And left the thorn wi' me.

AE FOND KISS, AND THEN WE SEVER

Ae fond kiss, and then we sever;
Ae fareweel, and then forever!
Deep in heart-wrung tears I'll pledge thee,
Warring sighs and groans I'll wage thee.
Who shall say that Fortune grieves him,
While the star of hope she leaves him?
Me, nae cheerful twinkle lights me;
Dark despair around benights me.

I'll ne'er blame my partial fancy,
Naething could resist my Nancy:
But to see her was to love her;
Love but her, and love for ever.
Had we never lov'd sae kindly,
Had we never lov'd sae blindly,
Never met—or never parted—
We had ne'er been broken-hearted.

Fare-thee-weel, thou first and fairest!
Fare-thee-weel, thou best and dearest!
Thine be ilka joy and treasure,
Peace, Enjoyment, Love and Pleasure!
Ae fond kiss, and then we sever!
Ae fareweel, alas, for ever!
Deep in heart-wrung tears I'll pledge thee,
Warring sighs and groans I'll wage thee.

It was a' for our rightfu' King
  We left fair Scotland's strand;
It was a' for our rightfu' King
  We e'er saw Irish land, my dear,
  We e'er saw Irish land.

Now a' is done that men can do,
  And a' is done in vain;
My Love and Native Land fareweel,
  For I maun cross the main, my dear,
  For I maun cross the main.

He turn'd him right and round about,
  Upon the Irish shore;
And gae his bridle reins a shake,
  With adieu for evermore, my dear,
  And adieu for evermore.

The soger frae the wars returns,
  The sailor frae the main;
But I hae parted frae my love,
  Never to meet again, my dear,
  Never to meet again.

When day is gane, and night is come,
  And a' folk bound to sleep;
I think on him that's far awa,
  The lee-lang night and weep, my dear,
  The lee-lang night and weep.

AY, WAUKIN, O

Chorus   Ay, waukin, O.
       Waukin still and wearie!
    Sleep I can get nane
       For thinking on my dearie.

SIMMER's a pleasant time;
    Flowers of ev'ry colour;
The water rins o'er the heugh,
    And I long for my true lover.

When I sleep I dream,
    When I wauk I'm eerie,
Sleep I can get nane
    For thinking on my dearie.

Lanely night comes on,
    A' the lave are sleepin,
I think on my bonie lad,
    And I blear my een wi' greetin.

UP IN THE MORNING EARLY

CAULD blaws the wind frae east to west,
    The drift is driving sairly;
Sae loud and shill's I hear the blast—
    I'm sure it's winter fairly.

Chorus   Up in the morning's no for me,
      Up in the morning early;
    When a' the hills are covered wi' snaw,
      I'm sure it's winter fairly.

    The birds sit chittering in the thorn,
      A' day they fare but sparely;
  And lang's the night frae e'en to morn—
      I'm sure it's winter fairly.

OF A' THE AIRTS THE WIND CAN BLAW

    Of a' the airts the wind can blaw,
      I dearly like the west,
  For there the bonie lassie lives,
      The lassie I lo'e best;
  There's wild-woods grow, and rivers row,
      And mony a hill between:
  But day and night my fancy's flight
      Is ever wi' my Jean.

    I see her in the dewy flowers,
      I see her sweet and fair:
  I hear her in the tunefu' birds,
      I hear her charm the air:
  There's not a bonie flower that springs,
      By fountain, shaw, or green;
  There's not a bonie bird that sings,
      But minds me o' my Jean.

O WERT thou in the cauld blast,
　On yonder lea, on yonder lea,
My plaidie to the angry airt,
　I'd shelter thee, I'd shelter thee;
Or did Misfortune's bitter storms
　Around thee blaw, around thee blaw,
Thy bield should be my bosom,
　To share it a', to share it a'.

Or were I in the wildest waste,
　Sae black and bare, sae black and bare,
The desert were a Paradise,
　If thou wert there, if thou wert there;
Or were I Monarch o' the globe,
　Wi' thee to reign, wi' thee to reign,
The brightest jewel in my Crown
　Wad be my Queen, wad be my Queen.

COMIN' THRO' THE RYE

Chorus　　O, Jenny's a' weet, poor body,
　　　　　　Jenny's seldom dry;
　　　　　She draigl't a' her petticoatie,
　　　　　　Comin' thro' the rye!

Comin' thro' the rye, poor body,
 Comin' thro' the rye,
She draigl't a' her petticoatie,
 Comin' thro' the rye!

Gin a body meet a body
 Comin' thro' the rye;
Gin a body kiss a body
 Need a body cry?

Gin a body meet a body
 Comin' thro' the glen;
Gin a body kiss a body
 Need the warld ken?

THE RIGS O' BARLEY

It was upon a Lammas night,
 When corn rigs are bonie,
Beneath the moon's unclouded light
 I held awa to Annie;
The time flew by, wi' tentless heed,
 Till, 'tween the late and early,
Wi' sma' persuasion she agreed
 To see me thro' the barley.

Chorus   Corn rigs, an' barley rigs,
   An' corn rigs are bonie:
  I'll ne'er forget that happy night,
   Amang the rigs wi' Annie.

The sky was blue, the wind was still,
  The moon was shining clearly;
I set her down, wi' right good will,
  Amang the rigs o' barley:
I ken't her heart was a' my ain;
  I lov'd her most sincerely;
I kiss'd her owre and owre again,
  Amang the rigs o' barley.

I lock'd her in my fond embrace;
  Her heart was beating rarely:
My blessings on that happy place,
  Amang the rigs o' barley!
But by the moon and stars so bright,
  That shone that hour so clearly!
She aye shall bless that happy night
  Amang the rigs o' barley.

I hae been blythe wi' comrades dear;
  I hae been merry drinking;
I hae been joyfu' gath'rin gear;
  I hae been happy thinking:
But a' the pleasures e'er I saw,
  Tho' three times doubl'd fairly,
That happy night was worth them a'
  Amang the rigs o' barley.

GREEN GROW THE RASHES, O

———

Chorus   Green grow the rashes, O;
          Green grow the rashes, O;
      The sweetest hours that e'er I spend,
         Are spent amang the lasses, O.

THERE's nought but care on ev'ry han',
   In ev'ry hour that passes, O:
What signifies the life o' man,
   An 'twere na for the lasses, O.

The war'ly race may riches chase,
   An' riches still may fly them, O;
An' tho' at last they catch them fast,
   Their hearts can ne'er enjoy them, O.

But gie me a cannie hour at e'en,
   My arms about my dearie, O;
An' war'ly cares, an' war'ly men,
   May a' gae tapsalteerie, O!

For you sae douce, ye sneer at this;
   Ye're nought but senseless asses, O:
The wisest man that warl' e'er saw,
   He dearly lov'd the lasses, O.

Auld Nature swears, the lovely dears
   Her noblest work she classes, O:
Her prentice han' she try'd on man,
   An' then she made the lasses, O.

I'M O'ER YOUNG TO MARRY YET

Chorus   I'm o'er young, I'm o'er young,
        I'm o'er young to marry yet;
    I'm o'er young, 'twad be a sin
        To tak me frae my mammy yet.

I AM my mammy's ae bairn,
    Wi' unco folk I weary, sir;
And lying in a man's bed,
    I'm fley'd it mak me eerie, sir.

My mammy coft me a new gown,
    The kirk maun hae the gracing o't;
Were I to lie wi' you, kind sir,
    I'm fear'd ye'd spoil the lacing o't.

Hallowmass is come and gane,
    The nights are lang in winter, sir,
And you an' I in ae bed,—
    In trowth, I dare na venture, sir.

Fu' loud an' shill the frosty wind
    Blaws thro' the leafless timmer, sir;
But if ye come this gate again,
    I'll aulder be gin simmer, sir.

DUNCAN DAVISON

THERE was a lass, they ca'd her Meg,
   And she held o'er the moors to spin;
There was a lad that follow'd her,
   They ca'd him Duncan Davison.
The moor was dreigh, and Meg was skeigh,
   Her favour Duncan could na win;
For wi' the rock she wad him knock,
   And aye she shook the temper-pin.

As o'er the moor they lightly foor,
   A burn was clear, a glen was green,
Upon the banks they eas'd their shanks,
   And aye she set the wheel between:
But Duncan swoor a haly aith,
   That Meg should be a bride the morn;
Then Meg took up her spinning-graith,
   And flang them a' out o'er the burn.

We will big a wee, wee house,
   And we will live like king and queen;
Sae blythe and merry's we will be,
   When ye set by the wheel at e'en.
A man may drink, and no be drunk;
   A man may fight, and no be slain;
A man may kiss a bonie lass,
   And aye be welcome back again!

DUNCAN GRAY

DUNCAN GRAY cam' here to woo,
  Ha, ha, the wooing o't,
On blythe Yule-night when we were fou,
  Ha, ha, the wooing o't:
Maggie coost her head fu' heigh,
Look'd asklent and unco skeigh,
Gart poor Duncan stand abeigh;
  Ha, ha, the wooing o't.

Duncan fleech'd and Duncan pray'd;
  Ha, ha, the wooing o't,
Meg was deaf as Ailsa craig,
  Ha, ha, the wooing o't:
Duncan sigh'd baith out and in,
Grat his e'en baith blear't an' blin',
Spak o' lowpin o'er a linn;
  Ha, ha, the wooing o't.

Time and Chance are but a tide,
  Ha, ha, the wooing o't,
Slighted love is sair to bide,
  Ha, ha, the wooing o't:
"Shall I like a fool," quoth he,
"For a haughty hizzie die?
She may gae to—France for me!"
  Ha, ha, the wooing o't.

How it comes let doctors tell,
  Ha, ha, the wooing o't;

Meg grew sick, as he grew hale,
   Ha, ha, the wooing o't.
Something in her bosom wrings,
For relief a sigh she brings:
And O! her een they spak sic things!
   Ha, ha, the wooing o't.

Duncan was a lad o' grace,
   Ha, ha, the wooing o't:
Maggie's was a piteous case,
   Ha, ha, the wooing o't:
Duncan could na be her death,
Swelling Pity smoor'd his wrath;
Now they're crouse and canty baith,
   Ha, ha, the wooing o't.

THE BRAW WOOER

———————

LAST May, a braw wooer cam doun the lang glen,
   And sair wi' his love he did deave me;
I said, there was naething I hated like men—
   The deuce gae wi'm to believe me, believe me;
   The deuce gae wi'm to believe me.

He spak o' the darts in my bonie black e'en,
   And vow'd for my love he was diein,
I said, he might die when he likèd for Jean—
   The Lord forgie me for liein, for liein;
   The Lord forgie me for liein!

A weel-stockèd mailen, himsel' for the laird,
　And marriage aff-hand, were his proffers;
I never loot on that I kenn'd it, or car'd;
　But thought I might hae waur offers, waur offers;
　But thought I might hae waur offers.

But what wad ye think?—in a fortnight or less
　(The deil tak his taste to gae near her!)
He up the Gate-Slack to my black cousin, Bess—
　Guess ye how, the jad! I could bear her, could bear her;
　Guess ye how, the jad! I could bear her.

But a' the niest week, as I petted wi' care,
　I gaed to the tryst o' Dalgarnock;
But wha but my fine fickle wooer was there,
　I glowr'd as I'd seen a warlock, a warlock,
　I glowr'd as I'd seen a warlock.

But owre my left shouther I gae him a blink,
　Lest neibours might say I was saucy;
My wooer he caper'd as he'd been in drink,
　And vow'd I was his dear lassie, dear lassie,
　And vow'd I was his dear lassie.

I spier'd for my cousin fu' couthy and sweet,
　Gin she had recover'd her hearin,
And how her new shoon fit her auld schachl't feet;
　But heavens! how he fell a swearing, a swearing,
　But heavens! how he fell a swearin.

He beggèd for gudesake, I wad be his wife,
　Or else I wad kill him wi' sorrow;
So e'en to preserve the poor body in life,
　I think I maun wed him to-morrow, to-morrow;
　I think I maun wed him to-morrow.

THERE'S A YOUTH IN THIS CITY

There's a youth in this city, it were a great pity
   That he from our lasses should wander awa';
For he's bonie and braw, weel-favor'd witha',
   An' his hair has a natural buckle an' a'.

His coat is the hue o' his bonnet sae blue,
   His fecket is white as the new-driven snaw;
His hose they are blae, and his shoon like the slae,
   And his clear siller buckles, they dazzle us a'.

For beauty and fortune the laddie's been courtin;
   Weel-featur'd, weel-tocher'd, weel-mounted an' braw;
But chiefly the siller that gars him gang till her,
   The penny's the jewel that beautifies a'.

There's Meg wi the mailen that fain wad a haen him,
   And Susie, wha's daddie was laird o' the Ha';
There's lang-tocher'd Nancy maist fetters his fancy,
   But the laddie's dear sel', he loes dearest of a'.

THE TARBOLTON LASSES

If ye gae up to yon hill-tap,
　Ye'll there see bonie Peggy;
She kens her father is a laird,
　And she forsooth's a leddy.

There's Sophy tight, a lassie bright,
　Besides a handsome fortune:
Wha canna win her in a night,
　Has little art in courtin.

Gae down by Faile, and taste the ale,
　And tak a look o' Mysie;
She's dour and din, a deil within,
　But aiblins she may please ye.

If she be shy, her sister try,
　Ye'll maybe fancy Jenny;
If ye'll dispense wi' want o' sense—
　She kens hersel she's bonie.

As ye gae up by yon hillside,
　Speir in for bonie Bessy;
She'll gie ye a beck, and bid ye light,
　And handsomely address ye.

There's few sae bonie, nane sae guid,
　In a' King George' dominion;
If ye should doubt the truth o' this—
　It's Bessy's ain opinion!

O LEAVE NOVÉLS

O LEAVE novéls, ye Mauchline belles,
　　Ye're safer at your spinning-wheel;
Such witching books are baited hooks
　　For rakish rooks like Rob Mossgiel.

Your fine *Tom Jones* and *Grandisons*,
　　They make your youthful fancies reel;
They heat your brains, and fire your veins,
　　And then you're prey for Rob Mossgiel.

Beware a tongue that's smoothly hung,
　　A heart that warmly seems to feel;
That feeling heart but acts a part—
　　'Tis rakish art in Rob Mossgiel.

The frank address, the soft caress,
　　Are worse than poisoned darts of steel;
The frank address, and politesse,
　　Are all finesse in Rob Mossgiel.

A LASS WI' A TOCHER

Awa' wi' your witchcraft o' Beauty's alarms,
The slender bit Beauty you grasp in your arms,
O, gie me the lass that has acres o' charms,
O, gie me the lass wi' the weel-stockit farms.

Chorus   Then hey, for a lass wi' a tocher,
            Then hey, for a lass wi' a tocher;
            Then hey, for a lass wi' a tocher;
                The nice yellow guineas for me.

Your Beauty's a flower, in the morning that blows,
And withers the faster, the faster it grows:
But the rapturous charm o' the bonie green knowes,
Ilk spring they're new deckit wi' bonie white yowes.

And e'en when this Beauty your bosom hath blest,
The brightest o' Beauty may cloy when possess'd;
But the sweet, yellow darlings wi' Geordie impress'd,
The langer ye hae them, the mair they're carest.

O WHISTLE AN' I'LL COME TO YE, MY LAD

Chorus   O whistle an' I'll come to ye, my lad,
            O whistle an' I'll come to ye, my lad,
            Tho' father an' mother an' a' should gae mad,
            O whistle an' I'll come to ye, my lad.

    But warily tent when ye come to court me,
    And come nae unless the back-yett be a-jee;
    Syne up the back-stile, and let naebody see,
    And come as ye were na comin to me,
    And come as ye were na comin to me.

    At kirk, or at market, whene'er ye meet me,
    Gang by me as tho' that ye car'd na a flie;

But steal me a blink o' your bonie black e'e,
Yet look as ye were na lookin to me,
Yet look as ye were na lookin to me.

Aye vow and protest that ye care na for me,
And whiles ye may lightly my beauty a-wee;
But court na anither, tho' jokin ye be,
For fear that she wyle your fancy frae me,
For fear that she wyle your fancy frae me.

WHA IS THAT AT MY BOWER-DOOR

"WHA is that at my bower-door?"
   "O wha is it but Findlay!"
"Then gae your gate, ye'se nae be here:"
   "Indeed maun I," quo' Findlay;
"What mak' ye, sae like a thief?"
   "O come and see," quo' Findlay;
"Before the morn ye'll work mischief:"
   "Indeed will I," quo' Findlay.

"Gif I rise and let you in"—
   "Let me in," quo' Findlay;
"Ye'll keep me waukin wi' your din:"
   "Indeed will I," quo' Findlay;
"In my bower if ye should stay"—
   "Let me stay," quo' Findlay;
"I fear ye'll bide till break o' day:"
   "Indeed will I," quo' Findlay.

"Here this night if ye remain"—
    "I'll remain," quo' Findlay;
"I dread ye'll learn the gate again:"
    "Indeed will I," quo' Findlay.
"What may pass within this bower"—
    "Let it pass," quo' Findlay;
"Ye maun conceal till your last hour:"
    "Indeed will I," quo' Findlay.

WHISTLE O'ER THE LAVE O'T

FIRST when Maggie was my care,
Heav'n, I thought, was in her air,
Now we're married—speir nae mair,
    But whistle o'er the lave o't!
Meg was meek, and Meg was mild,
Sweet and harmless as a child—
Wiser men than me's beguil'd;
    Whistle o'er the lave o't!

How we live, my Meg and me,
How we love, and how we gree,
I care na by how few may see—
    Whistle o'er the lave o't!
Wha I wish were maggot's meat,
Dish'd up in her winding-sheet,
I could write—but Meg maun see't—
    Whistle o'er the lave o't!

THE DEIL'S AWA WI' TH' EXCISEMAN

THE deil cam fiddlin thro' the town,
   And danc'd awa wi' th' Exciseman,
And ilka wife cries, "Auld Mahoun,
   I wish you luck o' the prize, man."

Chorus   The deil's awa, the deil's awa,
      The deil's awa wi' the Exciseman,
    He's danc'd awa, he's danc'd awa,
      He's danc'd awa wi' th' Exciseman.

We'll mak our maut, and we'll brew our drink,
   We'll laugh, sing, and rejoice, man,
And mony braw thanks to the meikle black deil,
   That danc'd awa wi' th' Exciseman.

There's threesome reels, there's foursome reels,
   There's hornpipes and strathspeys, man,
But the ae best dance ere came to the land
   Was "The deil's awa wi' th' Exciseman."

WILLIE BREW'D A PECK O' MAUT

O WILLIE brew'd a peck o' maut,
   And Rob and Allen cam to see;
Three blyther hearts, that lee-lang night,
   Ye wadna found in Christendie.

Chorus   We are na fou, we're nae that fou,
        But just a drappie in our ee;
      The cock may craw, the day may daw,
        And aye we'll taste the barley bree.

Here are we met, three merry boys,
    Three merry boys I trow are we;
And mony a night we've merry been,
    And mony mae we hope to be!

It is the moon, I ken her horn,
    That's blinkin' in the lift sae hie;
She shines sae bright to wile us hame,
    But, by my sooth, she'll wait a wee!

Wha first shall rise to gang awa,
    A cuckold, coward loun is he!
Wha first beside his chair shall fa',
    He is the King amang us three.

AULD LANG SYNE

———

SHOULD auld acquaintance be forgot,
    And never brought to mind?
Should auld acquaintance be forgot,
    And auld lang syne!

Chorus   For auld lang syne, my dear,
        For auld lang syne,
      We'll tak a cup o' kindness yet,
        For auld lang syne.

And surely ye'll be your pint stowp!
    And surely I'll be mine!
And we'll tak a cup o' kindness yet,
    For auld lang syne.

We twa hae run about the braes,
    And pou'd the gowans fine;
But we've wander'd mony a weary fit,
    Sin' auld lang syne.

We twa hae paidl'd in the burn,
    Frae morning sun till dine;
But seas between us braid hae roar'd
    Sin' auld lang syne.

And there's a hand, my trusty fere!
    And gie's a hand o' thine!
And we'll tak' a right gude-willie waught,
    For auld lang syne.

JOHN ANDERSON, MY JO

JOHN ANDERSON, my jo, John,
    When we were first acquent;
Your locks were like the raven,
    Your bonie brow was brent;
But now your brow is beld, John,
    Your locks are like the snow;
But blessings on your frosty pow,
    John Anderson, my jo.

John Anderson, my jo, John,
   We clamb the hill thegither;
And mony a cantie day, John,
   We've had wi' ane anither:
Now we maun totter down, John,
   And hand in hand we'll go,
And sleep thegither at the foot,
   John Anderson, my jo.

SCOTS, WHA HAE

———

Scots, wha hae wi' WALLACE bled,
Scots, wham BRUCE has aften led,
Welcome to your gory bed,
            Or to victorie!

Now's the day, and now's the hour;
See the front o' battle lour;
See approach proud EDWARD's power—
            Chains and slaverie!

Wha will be a traitor knave?
Wha can fill a coward's grave?
Wha sae base as be a slave?
            Let him turn and flee!

Wha, for Scotland's King and Law,
Freedom's sword will strongly draw,
Free-man stand, or Free-man fa',
            Let him on wi' me!

By Oppression's woes and pains!
By your sons in servile chains!
We will drain our dearest veins,
But they shall be free!

Lay the proud Usurpers low!
Tyrants fall in every foe!
Liberty's in every blow!—
Let us do or die!

A MAN'S A MAN FOR A' THAT

Is there for honest poverty
That hings his head, an' a' that;
The coward slave—we pass him by,
We dare be poor for a' that!
For a' that, an' a' that,
Our toils obscure an' a' that,
The rank is but the guinea's stamp,
The man's the gowd for a' that.

What though on hamely fare we dine,
Wear hoddin grey, an' a' that?
Gie fools their silks, and knaves their wine,
A man's a man for a' that.
For a' that, an' a' that,
Their tinsel show, an' a' that,
The honest man, tho' e'er sae poor,
Is king o' men for a' that.

Ye see yon birkie ca'd a lord,
    Wha struts, an' stares, an' a' that;
Tho' hundreds worship at his word,
    He's but a coof for a' that.
For a' that, an' a' that,
    His ribband, star, an' a' that,
The man o' independent mind
    He looks an' laughs at a' that.

A prince can mak a belted knight,
    A marquis, duke, an' a' that;
But an honest man's aboon his might,
    Gude faith, he maunna fa' that!
For a' that, an' a' that,
    Their dignities an' a' that,
The pith o' sense, an' pride o' worth,
    Are higher rank than a' that.

Then let us pray that come it may,
    (As come it will for a' that,)
That Sense and Worth, o'er a' the earth,
    Shall bear the gree, an' a' that.
For a' that, an' a' that,
    It's coming yet for a' that,
That man to man, the world o'er,
    Shall brithers be for a' that.

GLOSSARY

a', all
abeigh, aloof
aboon, above
abread, abroad
acquent, acquainted
ae, one, only
aff, off
aft, aften, oft, often
agley, awry
aiblins, perhaps
ain, own
airn, iron
airt, direction
aith, oath
ajee, ajar
amang, among
an', and, if
ance, once
ane, one
anither, another
asklent, askew
auld, old
aumous, alms
ava', of all, at all
awa', away
awee, a short time; disparage
ayont, beyond

bairn, child
baith, both
bake, biscuit
bane, bone
bannock, a cake of oatmeal or
    barley
barefit, barefoot
barmie, yeasty
bauckie-bird, bat
bauld, bold

be (sometimes), pay for
bear, barley
beck, curtsey
beld, bald
belyve, by and by
ben, into the parlor
benmost, innermost
bent, open field
bethankit, grace after meat
beuk, book
bide, stay
biel', bield, shelter
big, to build
bill, bull
billie, fellow
birk, birch
birkie, smart fellow
bit, small
bizz, to buzz
blae, blue
blastie, blasted wretch
blastit, blasted
blather, bladder
blaw, blawn, blow, blown
blear't, blearit, dim
bleeze, blaze; to blaze
blellum, babbler
blether, to talk nonsense
blin', blind
blink, glance
blinkit, leered
bluid, blude, blood
blume, bloom
boddle, tuppence (Scots)
bogle, bogilis, hobgoblin(s)
bonie, bonny
boord, board
boor-tree, elder tree

bore, hole, small opening
botch, blotch
bouse, bowse, drink
brae, bank
braid, broad
brak, broke
brattle, spurt, scamper
braw, brave, handsome
breef, brief, writ; spell
breeks, breeches
brent, smooth, steep
brent-new, brand-new
brig, bridge
brither, brother
brogue, trick
brownlis, brownies
brunstane, brimstone
buckle, curl
buke, book
bum, buttocks; to hum
bummin, humming
burdies, lasses
burn, a small stream
but, without, wanting
butt, but, in the kitchen (see **ben**)
byke, hive, swarm

ca', call; drive
cadger, hawker, carrier
caff, chaff
caird, tinker
cairn, pile of stones, hill
callan, callant, boy, stripling
caller, fresh, cool
callet, trull
cam, came
canna, cannot
cannie, knowing
cannily, cannalie, softly
cantie, cheerful, merry

cantraip, cantrip, spell, magic
cape-stane, capstone
carl, old man, churl
carlin, old woman
cartes, playing cards
cauld, cold
caup, wooden cup
cavie, coop
change house, inn
chapman, peddler
chiel', fellow
chittering, shivering
chuck, chuckie, hen, dear
cit, citizen
claes, claise, clothes
claith, cloth
claithing, clothing
clamb, climbed
clap, clapper of a mill
clash, idle talk
clatter, talk, gossip
claw, scratch
claymore, two-handed sword
cleek, snatch
cleekit, joined hands
clink down, sit down quickly
clinkum-bell, bell ringer
cloot, hoof
Clootie, the devil
clout, patch
clunk, to sound
co'er, cover
coft, bought
cog, coggie, wooden cup
coof, blockhead
coost, cast, threw off
cootie, small dish; rough-legg**èd**
core, gang
cotter, cottar, cottager
countra, country

cour, stoop
couthie, kind
crack, conversation
craig, craigie, throat, neck
cranreuch, hoarfrost
craw, crow
creeshie, greasy
croon, moan
cross, across
crouded, crowded
crouse, elated
crowdie, porridge
crowlin, crawling
crummock, crooked staff
crump, crisp
curchie, curtsy
cutes, ankles
cutty, short
cutty-stool, stool of repentance

daffin, merrymaking
daft, mad, foolish
dails, planks
daimen, odd
daud, large piece
daur, dare
dautie, dawtit, darling
daw, dawn
deave, deafen
deckit, decked out
deil, devil
deil's a boddle, two cents'
  worth
dight, wipe
din, dark-skinned
ding, beat, surpass
dinna, do not
dirl, rattle
doited, stupefied
donsie, restive, unlucky
dool, woe

douce, douse, grave, gentle,
  sedate
douk, duck
doun, down
doup, backside
dour, stubborn
dow, be able
dowie, doleful
doxy, paramour
doytin, straggling
draigl't, draggled
drap, drappie, drop
dreepin, dripping
dreigh, wearisome
dribble, drizzle
driddle, toddle
droddum, breech
drouth, thirst
drouthy, thirsty
drumlie, muddy
dub, puddle
duddie, ragged
duddies, clothes
dwalt, dwelt
dyke, wall

e'e, eye
e'en, eyes
e'er, ere, ever
eerie, ghostly, strange
eild, old age
eldritch, unearthly, hideous
Erse, Gaelic
ettle, aim, intent

fa', fall
fae, foe
fain, fond
fair-fa', good befall
fairin, reward
fairy, small

fand, found
farls, oatcakes
fash, trouble
fatt'rels, trimmings
faun, fallen
fause, false
faut, fault
fecht, fight
feck, greater part, value
fecket, vest
feckless, weak
fend, depend
fere, comrade
ferlie, wonder, marvel
fient a, not a
fit, foot
flainen, flannel
flang, kicked
fleech, beg
fley, scare
flie, fly
foggage, coarse grass
foor, went
foord, ford
forgie, forgive
fou, full, drunk
foughten, troubled
frae, from
fu', full
fud, tail
furms, wooden forms
furr, furrow
fyke, bustle
fyle, dirty

gab, mouth; to talk
gae, gang, go
gaed, went
gane, gone
gangrel, vagrant
gar, make, cause

gat, got
gate, way
gates, ways, habits
gaud, goad
gaun, going
gausy, gawsy, jolly
gear, wealth
get, offspring
ghaist, ghost
gie, give
gif, if
giglets, girls
gillie, gill
gin, by the time of; if
girdle, griddle
girn, snarl
gizz, wig
glaikit, foolish
glint, glance
gloamin, twilight
glow'r, stare; glowering
gooms, gums
gowan, daisy
gowd, gold
graith, gear
grat, wept
graunie, granny
gree, prize
greet, weep
grozet, gooseberry
grun, ground
gude, guid, good
gudesake, god's sake
gude-willie, hearty
guidman, head of household

ha', hall
hae, have
haen, had
hafflins-wise, by halves
haggis, pudding of entrails

hainch, hip
hal', hald, holding
hale, whole
haly, holy
hame, home
hamely, homely
hangie, hangman
han's, hands
hap, covering
happer, hopper
harn, coarse cloth
haud, hold
havins, good manners
hawkie, cow
heigh, high
held awa, went off
het, hot
heugh, hollow pit
hie, high
hing, hang
hirple, limp
histie, bare
hizzie, hussy
hoddin, riding heavily; rough cloth
hoolie, softly
hoord, hoard
horn, horn spoon, comb
Hornie, Satan
host, cough
hotch'd, fidgeted
houghmagandie, byplay
houlet, owl
houp, hope
howe, hollow
howk, dig
hunder, hundred
hunkers, haunches
hurcheon, hedgehog
hurchin, urchin
hurdies, buttocks

icker, ear of corn
ilk, ilka, each, every
ingle, fireplace
ither, other

jad, jade
jaup, splash
jinkin, dodging
jouk, duck
jow, swing and toll

kail, kale, cabbage
kebars, rafters
kebbuck, cheese
keckle, giggle
keepit, kept
ken, know
kennin, very little
ket, fleece
kiltit, hitched up
kin', kind
kirn, churn
kirtle, small skirt
kittle, ticklish, fickle
knowe, knoll, hillock
kyte, belly

lade, load
lag, backward, slow
laird, squire
laith, loath
lallan', lowland
lan', land
lane, alone
lanely, lonely
lang, long
langer, longer
lap, leaped
lave, the rest
lav'rock, lark
lea'e, leave

lear, learning
lee-lang, livelong
leeze me, blessings (on)
leuk, look
lift, sky
lin, linn, waterfall
link, trip quickly
lo'e, love
loof, palm of the hand
loon, loun, fellow
loot, let
lough, pond
loup, lowp, leap
lour, impending
lowin, blazing
lowse, untie
lug, ear; corner
luggie, wooden dish
lunardi, balloon-bonnet, named
     after balloonist Lunardi
lunch, large portion
luve, love
lyart, gray, faded

mae, more
Mahoun, Satan
mailen, farm
Mailie, Molly
mair, more
'maist, 'most, almost
mak, make
'mang, among
manteele, mantle
maukin, hare
maun, must
maunna, must not
maut, malt
meikle, much, great
melder, grinding of corn
mell, meddle
men', mend

mense, manners
menseless, unmannerly
midden, dunghill
mim, prim
mind, remind
mirk, dark
mither, mother
mony, many
mools, earth dust
moop, consort, meddle
moss, bog
muckle, big, great
muir, moor
muslin-kail, thin broth

na, not
nae, no
naething, nothing
naig, nag
nane, none
nappy, ale
neebor, neibor, neighbor
neist, next
neuk, corner
Nickie-ben, devil
nieve, fist
niffer, exchange
nighted, benighted
nit, nut
no to, not to
noddle, brain

o', of
ony, any
orra, extra
oursels, ourselves
owre, over

paidle, paddle
painch, paunch
pang, cram

pattle, plough stick
pawkie, sly, artful
penny wheep, small ale
philibeg, kilt
phiz, face
pin, skewer
pint-stoup, vessel containing
    two English quarts
pit, put
plaisters, plasters
pliver, plover
pock, bag, wallet
pou, pu', pull, gather
pow, poll, head
prent, print
press, cupboard
propone, propose
pund Scots, Scots pound
pussie, hare
pyke, pick
pyles, grains

quaick, quack
quat, quit
quean, girl

rade, rode
raible, recite by rote
raip, rape, rope
rair, roar
ram-stam, headlong
randie, quarrelsome, rascal
rant, roister
rantin, lively
rash, rush
rash-buss, clump of rushes
ratton, rat
raucle, rough
raw, row
ream, froth
reave, rob

red, advise
reekit, smoky
reestit, smoked
remead, remedy
rief, robbery
rig, ridge of land
rigwoodie, bony, lean
rin, run
ripp, handful
rive, tear, burst
rousty, rusty
routh, rowth, abundance
row, rowe, flow
rozet, rosin
runkl'd, wrinkled
ryke, reach

sae, so
saft, soft
sair, sore
sang, song
sark, shirt
saul, soul
saunt, saint
saut, salt
sax, six
scaud, scald
scaul', scold
scaur, frightened
sconner, disgust
screed, rip, rent
scrimpit, scanty
session, court
shachl't, shapeless
shavie, trick
sheuk, shook
shill, shrill
shog, shake
shoon, shoes
shore, threaten
shouther, shoulder

sic, such
siller, money, silver
silly, frail
simmer, summer
sin', since
skeigh, skittish
skellum, rascal
skelp, slap
skelpin, resounding
skinking, thin, watery
skirl, scream
sklent, slant; deviate
skriech, screech
skyte, dash
slae, sloe
slap, opening
slee'st, slyest
sleekit, sleek
sma', small
smeddum, powder
smoor, smother
smoutie, smutty
snakin, sneering
snaw, snow
sned, cut, lop
snell, bitter
snick, latch
snirtle, snigger
sodger, soger, soldier
sonsie, jolly
sough, sighing sound
souple, supple
souter, cobbler
spairge, spatter
spak, spoke
spavie, spavin
spean, wean
speel, climb
speer, speir, ask
speet, impale
spence, parlor

splore, frolic, uproar
spontoon, half-pike
spreckl'd, speckled
spunkie, will-o'-the-wisp
squatter, flap
squattle, sprawl
stack, stuck
stane, stone
stang, sting
stank, stagnant pool
stan's, stands
stap, stop
staw, stole
steer, stir
stibble, stubble
stirk, bullock
stoiter, stagger
stoor, stern
stot, ox
stour, dust, turmoil
stowp, pot
strang, strong
strathspey, dance, reel
strunt, liquor; strut
swaird, sward
swat, sweated
swatch, sample
swats, ale
swith, quick
swoor, swore
syne, then, since

taen, taken
taets, small quantities
tak, take
tap, top
tapsalteerie, topsy-turvy
tauld, told
tauted, tawted, matted
temper pin, fiddle peg

tend, tent, heed
tentless, heedless
teuk, took
thae, those
thairm, fiddlestring
thegither, together
thir, these
thole, suffer, endure
thowe, thaw
thrang, throng; busy, thick
thrave, twenty-four sheaves
thraw, twist, turn
thrissle, thistle
till, toward
till't, to it
timmer, timber
tinkler-hizzy, tinker wench
tint, lost
tip, ram
tippence, tuppence
tippenny, twopenny ale
tirlin, stripping
tither, the tither, the other
tittlin, whispering
tocher, dowry
toom, empty
toop, ram
tousie, touzie, shaggy
tout, blow
tow, rope
towmond, twelvemonth
towsing, tumbling
tozie, muddled
transmugrified, changed
trews, trousers
trow, trowth, truth, trust
tryste, market
trysted, prearranged
twa, two
twal', twelve
tyke, dog

unco, great, strange
unfald, unfold
unkend, unknown
upo', upon
usquebae, whisky

vauntie, proud
vera, very

wa', wall
wabster, weaver
wad, would
wadna, would not
wae, woe; sad
wae worth, woe befall
waesucks, alas
wale, choice; to choose
walie, large, stout
wallopèd, rushed
wanchancie, unlucky
wanrestfu', restless
wark, work
wark-lume, tool
warlock, wizard
warl's, world's
warst, worst
warstle, wrestle
wa's, walls
water-brose, oatmeal and
  water
water-kelpie, water spirit
waught, draught
wauk, wake
wauken, awaken
waukin, watching, waking
waulie, jolly
waur, worse
wave, weave
weary fa', plague upon
weel, well
weel-gaun, well-going

weel-tochered, well-dowered
weet, set; wet
we'se, we shall
wha, who
wham, whom
whang, slice
whar, whare, whaur, where (are)
whase, whose
whins, furze
whunstane, granite
whyles, sometimes
wi', with
wight, sturdy person
winna, will not
winnock-bunker, window seat
win's, winds
wist, guessed
wit, know

witha', withal
wonner, wonder
woo', wool
woodie, withy; gallows
wordy, worthy
wrang, wrong
wyle, entice
wyliecoat, vest

yard, garden
yell, dry, without milk
yerkit, jerked
yestreen, last night
yett, gate
yill, ale
yill-caup, alecup
yird, earth
yont, beyond
yowe, ewe

INDEX OF TITLES

133

INDEX OF FIRST LINES

ABOUT THE COMPILER

LLOYD FRANKENBERG is a well-known poet, critic, lecturer, and anthologist. A recipient of Guggenheim, Carnegie, Rockefeller, and Fulbright grants (among others), Mr. Frankenberg was director of poetry evenings at the Museum of Modern Art in New York City and originated a radio series entitled "What is Poetry About?" on WNYC.

Mr. Frankenberg's poems have appeared in book form (*The Red Kite*) and in numerous magazines and anthologies. He is the author of *Pleasure Dome: On Reading Modern Poetry* and has compiled three anthologies: *Invitation to Poetry; A James Stephens Reader;* and *James, Seumas and Jacques* (unpublished writings of James Stephens).

In addition, he has edited a recording of *Pleasure Dome: An Audible Anthology of Modern Poetry Read by Its Creators,* and to accompany *Invitation to Poetry* he has recorded a selection of poems and comments under the title *A Round of Poems.*

Mr. Frankenberg is married to the painter Loren MacIver and lives in New York and Paris.

ABOUT THE ILLUSTRATOR

JOSEPH LOW was born in Coraopolis, Pennsylvania; attended schools in Oak Park, Illinois; and studied at the University of Illinois. Finding that he could learn more of what he wanted by studying on his own in museums and libraries, he pursued his interest in the graphic arts, teaching himself the skills that he needed and acquiring the necessary tools, type, and a press.

After spending some time at the Art Students League in New York City, Mr. Low taught graphic arts at Indiana University for three years. He is a printer and publisher, with his own Eden Hill Press, as well as an artist.

His work has been exhibited in museums across the United States, in England, South America, Asia, and Europe. He lives in Connecticut with his wife and two daughters.